CONVERSATIONS WITH...
JESUS OF NAZARETH

CONVERSATIONS WITH...
JESUS OF NAZARETH

BY JESUS OF NAZARETH
WITH SIMON PARKE

WHITE CROW

Conversations with… Jesus of Nazareth

White Crow Books is an imprint of
White Crow Productions Ltd
PO Box 1013
Guildford GU1 9EJ

www.whitecrowbooks.com

Text design and eBook production by Essential Works
www.essentialworks.co.uk

Hardback ISBN 978-1-907661-43-3
Paperback ISBN 978-1-907661-41-9
eBook ISBN 978-1-907661-42-6
Audiobook ISBN 978-1-907661-62-4

Religion & Spirituality

Distributed in the UK by
Lightning Source Ltd.
Chapter House
Pitfield
Kiln Farm
Milton Keynes MK11 3LW

Distributed in the USA by
Lightning Source Inc.
246 Heil Quaker Boulevard
LaVergne
Tennessee 37086

Contents

Preface

The conversation presented here is imagined; but Jesus's words are not. All of Jesus's words included here are his own, taken mainly from the gospels of Matthew, Mark, Luke, John, and Thomas; though I have briefly visited those of Mary Magdalene and Phillip as well.

Seasoned Jesus-watchers will recognize that I have sometimes added link words to aid the flow; and on one or two occasions, put a story about Jesus into the first person, and placed it in his mouth.

Whatever your view of Jesus – and everyone has one – I trust that you will find here, in clear and startling focus, Jesus the man; for to find that man is the reason for this adventure. I have no desire to offend; only illumine. So here are his passions, his conflicts, his insights, his life, and his words.

Let us go now to the hot streets of Jerusalem...

Introduction

It is through an intermediary, a woman called Susanna, that Jesus of Nazareth has agreed to meet me, though who knows what I can expect? People are beginning to use rather flowery language to describe him, but whether it's justified, I'm not sure. I'm a gentile myself and much-travelled, but have lived among the Jews long enough to know that another starry-eyed messiah is no particular surprise.

The rumours around this man are many, with unconfirmed reports of a virgin birth, divine origins, dangerous teachings, and miracles of healing. Some even claim that he's been killed here in Jerusalem and is now alive again, so we must add 'resurrection' to the hearsay. But let us not be hasty. For me, you know them by their fruits, and I'm looking for the real Jesus, rather than a Jesus defined by others. What is the true nature of his message? And more importantly, what is the true nature of the man?

He speaks as one who has authority; this I hear again and again. What does that mean? I suppose it means that unlike many teachers, he and his message authenticate themselves in people's hearts, through their power to awaken things; to reach the hidden and courageous parts of the human soul and mind. It appears he doesn't want followers who hang on his every word; but rather, people who've dismantled their certainties, overturned their pasts, jettisoned possessions, and thrown away their fears. Only people such as these can walk in his footsteps, which suggests his following will always be small.

Some have used the word 'messiah', but they had best be wary, for this region is not favourable to those claiming that title, and perhaps a little history may be helpful here. Palestine, where I now sit, lies near the eastern confines of the Roman Empire. Jews are the dominant group and the Romans, who have never understood them, will tell you how stubborn they are. The nationalist revival two centuries ago is remembered like it was yesterday, and with much nostalgia by some. The zealots – political activists – represent such hopes, passionate in their desire to overthrow this hated Roman rule.

The priestly aristocracy, called Sadducees, hate the zealots. When do the rich ever want change? The zealots call the Sadducees Rome's bootlickers; and the Romans call the zealots bandits. All in all, Palestine is an unsettled place, with the balance of good and evil noticeably disturbed.

And yet, suddenly the followers of Jesus seem cheerful. Why? They claim this Jesus of Nazareth died and has come back to life. It sounds like a fine delusion, but they're so excited they run everywhere, quite unable to walk sensibly. It's all very puzzling. I met one or two of these folk before these events, and believe me, they were far from impressive. 'Just your average stupid Galileans,' as one religious leader told me, and it was hard to disagree.

So I'm interested to meet the man at the centre of this storm. Jesus – formerly Joshua bar Joseph – has agreed to speak, and in preparation, I've put my ear to the ground and met associates and onlookers alike. Matthew speaks a bit like a textbook, but has all sorts of stories; Luke's more of an individual, but shares many of Matthew's tales. They don't always quite agree – who does? – yet give a good sense of the sort of person Jesus is, the sort of things he does, the sort of things he says and, interestingly, the sort of people who find him disturbing. Thomas is different, of course. He tells me nothing about the life of Jesus, but is well-versed in his terse and unsettling teaching.

And then there's Mark, who is different again, more breathless in his account than anyone else. He can't keep still for a moment and nor does his story. He likes action, mainly, with Jesus doing this, and then that, and then something else, while John, well – that's not a meeting I'll forget. It was like the life of Jesus had already become a meditation for him, a mystical journey impregnated with meaning. He's wonderfully original in his take on things, and on another day I could have listened to him for hours. As a journalist, however, I just want the prosaic facts, and there's some disentangling to do before you get those from John.

And then there were the two Marys – his close friend Mary Magdalene and his mother Mary. Some say Magdalene was too close, and I'll raise that matter with him, but whatever the truth, these women offer a rather different take on the man; personal accounts, unlike those of onlookers like Pliny and Josephus who are informed and serious, but rely more on hearsay. They want to put the teacher in context, but haven't actually met the teacher themselves. It's a different sort of knowing.

But that's enough preparation. It's time to meet the man, which is why I'm walking towards the marketplace now. Some say there's a religion growing around him, but I'm not greatly concerned about that. Religions are twopenny, and often worth rather less. I'm interested in the religion *of* Jesus, rather than any religion *about* him. What will I find? Believe me, it's with a certain caution that I approach my conversation with...Jesus of Nazareth.

ONE

Are you political or spiritual?

---

*We meet in a Jerusalem marketplace. Jesus appears to want
anonymity, remaining hidden from public gaze, inside a basket
weaver's tent. Indeed, I don't see him well myself. Bread, olives,
fish, and wine appear at various times, provided by a couple of
attentive women, as outside, the day begins to fade. Around us are
the children of stall-holders, playing the day away in rather noisy
fashion; they're noisier than is helpful, and one or two wish to
come into the tent itself!*

SP: I'm sorry about the children; I had hoped for a bit of quiet.

JN: No, let the children come to me.

SP: I wouldn't encourage them, believe me. They can be like
honey in the hair, sweet but clinging.

JN: Whoever receives one such little child in my name receives
me.

SP: What extraordinary words, teacher.

JN: Then if you have ears, hear.

SP: I do have ears, teacher, but with all due respect, they're
slightly ridiculous words you speak. I mean, we all have a
regard for children, but they're not to be taken seriously,
surely, until they become adults?

JN: Most certainly I tell you, unless you turn and become as a
little child, you will in no way enter the kingdom of heaven.

SP: 'Unless I become as a child' – you mean, become like *them*? That's a strange choice of hero – particularly the noisy one over there pretending to be a donkey.

JN: Whoever humbles himself as that little child is the greatest in the kingdom of heaven.

SP: I see. So children are the pinnacle of human development? That's certainly different. I've heard nothing similar to that in the mouth of any other rabbi.

JN: And whoever causes one of these little ones to stumble, it would be better for them if a huge millstone was hung around their neck, and they were sunk deep in the sea.

SP: I have no wish that they should stumble, of course, but to take them quite so seriously? I mean, they hardly know what they're doing.

JN: Did you never read?

SP: Read what?

JN: 'Out of the mouth of babes and nursing babes you have perfected praise.'

SP: Perhaps I can glimpse what you're saying, teacher. There's innocence in childhood which we lose; something essential and true that is somehow conditioned out of us by life. Is that what you see?

JN: See that you don't despise any of these little ones.

SP: No, of course not.

JN: They have angels, I tell you.

SP: Really?

JN: They have angels, always, in the presence of my father in heaven.

SP: You talk as though this is your passion. It's no one else's passion, I can assure you. I just wonder why children are quite so important for you.

JN: The kingdom of heaven is like a treasure hidden in the field, which a man found and then hid. In his joy, he goes and sells all that he has, and buys that field.

SP: What are you saying? That children possess something which adults lose; and that to regain it, to get back to that place, is worth whatever it costs? Is that the secret?

JN: Or again, the kingdom of heaven is like a merchant seeking fine pearls, who having found a single pearl of great value, sells all he has to obtain it.

SP: You speak in riddles, teacher, I had heard this of you; so you must allow me thinking time and many questions. The man sells all he has?

JN: Sells all he has to obtain the pearl.

SP: That suggests that whatever it is we need – the recovery of such innocence and openness – is a hard thing to gain, and requires the letting go of much that is precious to us.

JN: If your foot causes you to stumble, then cut it off.

SP: Well, there's a picture!

JN: Better to enter life without a foot than to keep both feet and enter hell and the fires that never go out.

SP: But people don't like letting go, teacher. We are hoarders of our habits, bad or otherwise, so that's never going to be a popular teaching, not even if you stood –

JN: – I stood in the midst of the world.

SP: You did, yes.

JN: I appeared to them in flesh.

SP: And few who meet you forget you, teacher; there are many admiring witnesses to your life.

JN: But I found them all drunk.

SP: Drunk?

JN: I found none among them who were thirsting.

SP: You mean you found no one passionate for the truth?

JN: And my soul grieves for these people, for they are blind in their hearts and they do not see.

SP: What don't they see?

JN: Naked they came into the world and naked will they leave it.

SP: And in between, they clothe themselves with illusion?

JN: For now they are drunk, yes. But when they have vomited up their wine, perhaps then they will return to themselves.'

SP: You speak like a 'Moshel Meshalim,' a master of wisdom and not a politician. Yet I've spoken to some who were hoping you were such a man, one who would overthrow the Romans and restore national pride. You must have met such people too?

JN: There were two men going to the village of Emmaus.

SP: I know the place; a two-hour walk north from here.

JN: I approached them and walked with them for a while. I said to them, 'What are you talking about as you walk and why are sad?'

SP: They were unhappy about something?

JN: One of them, Cleopas, says, 'Are you the only stranger in Jerusalem who doesn't know the things which have happened there in these days?' I say 'What things?' and they say 'The whole business with Jesus of Nazareth, who was a powerful prophet in deed and word and how the chief priests and authorities had him condemned to death and crucified, while *we* were hoping he was the one to save Israel.'

SP: That's just what I mean; they thought you were the one to save Israel from the Romans.

JN: But my kingdom is not of this world.

SP: No, but whether you like it or not, you're linked by some

15

to John the Baptizer and he's linked to the zealots, so people put two and two together and make five. I actually heard John preaching once. A few of us took a day's trek out into the wilderness to see what the fuss was about. There were quite a few of us who came from Jerusalem.

JN: And what did you go out into the wilderness to see?

SP: What did we go to see? I don't know really. We'd just heard –

JN: – a reed shaken by the wind?

SP: John wasn't shaken by anyone. He was thundering on about putting an axe to the tree when I saw him.

JN: But what did you go out to see? A man clothed in soft clothing? Those who dress gorgeously and live delicately, such people live in royal palaces.

SP: Yes, I heard he was upsetting Herod Antipas, the governor of Galilee. And the zealots loved that, of course, because they hated Herod as a stooge of Rome.

JN: But what did you go out to see?

SP: A prophet, I suppose.

JN: A prophet?

SP: He had such passion. We hadn't seen that for a while; a real prophet at last, calling everyone to order!

JN: Yes, and I tell you, much more than a prophet.

s p : I'm not sure you can be *more* than a prophet.

j n : This John is the one of whom it is written, 'Look! I send my messenger to your door, who will prepare your way before you.'

s p : So you revere John the Baptizer. Yet the truth is, teacher, you didn't spend time with him, and seem to have gone your own way, really. You only spoke up for him after his execution in the hilltop fortress of Machaerus – as ordered by Herod.

j n : That fox.

s p : It was hardly a surprise though. Everyone knows that Galilee is a hotbed of Jewish unrest; the region is famous for it. In Galilee, religion and politics are one and the same, and I suppose John frightened him.

j n : Does anyone ever light a lamp and place it under a bowl or under the bed?

s p : Well, no, but the thing is, teacher, John seemed to think he could force things; force things with his harsh words and ascetic lifestyle. Here was a man dressed in camel hair and leather belt, who lived on locusts and wild honey. He told people to turn away from their sins.

j n : Pay attention to what you hear.

s p : But there was a lot of violence in his preaching of the kingdom; that was my impression. Is the kingdom violent?

j n : No, the kingdom of the father is like the dough in which a woman has hidden some yeast; it is changed into good bread.

sp: Your imagery is more peaceful than John's. The slow-rising dough is rather different from the axe being put to a tree, which was one of his favourite images.

jn: Yet I tell you, among those born of women, there is not a greater prophet than John the Baptizer.

sp: So you say.

jn: And then again, the one who is least in the kingdom of God is greater than he!

sp: Ah, there you go again, speaking in riddles. Somehow, John's both the best and the least. But can we just clear up your politics, teacher, for you are a Galilean and people do want to know your views?

jn: Show me a denarius.

sp: You know what I'm going to ask? Well, I suppose the tax-test is familiar enough. The zealots want to know if you think people should pay taxes to Rome, and I have a coin here.

jn: So whose image and inscription are on it?

sp: Caesar's Roman head is very clear.

jn: Then give to Caesar the things that are Caesar's, and to God the things that are God's.

sp: The Romans will like that answer; but you've just lost the zealots.

TWO

Why do you upset people?

They say the style is the man, and Jesus's style is short and crisp. With him, language is a force – pungent, earthy, sometimes cryptic, and piled high with paradox. He uses parable, hyperbole, aphorism, and irony. He hits the nail on the head, and then moves on.

As we talk, I'm struck by how often his words and attitudes resemble those of Rabbi Hillel the Elder, the great sage who died recently. Like Jesus, he was regarded by some as a dangerous radical. Hillel wished to humanize the religious laws and held sway in Jerusalem for a while; but it was his opponent Rabbi Shammai who took control after Hillel's death in 10AD. And it is these stricter Shammaites, in collusion with the Sadducees, who hound Jesus. Perhaps they see too much of Hillel in him.

Jerusalem is a bloody city, of course, a city full of hate. And as I sit now, picking at the olives, I'm suddenly aware of the three forces at work around me. Rome stands for order; the priests and Pharisees for institutional religion; and the zealots for patriotism. All good things in their way, you might say; yet Jesus upset them all. Why?

JN: Tell, me, what do you think?

SP: About what?

JN: A man had two sons, and he came to the first, and said, 'Son, go work today in my vineyard.' He answered, 'I will not,' but later changed his mind, and went.

SP: OK.

JN: The father then came to the second son, and said the same thing. 'Son, go and work in my vineyard.' He answered, 'I go, sir,' but then didn't go.

SP: Not unknown.

JN: Indeed. But which of the two did the will of his father?

SP: Well, the first, of course. But it's stories like this which unsettle the religious establishment and maybe this isn't a surprise. Your mother told me what Simeon the priest said when he blessed you as a child. 'This child is chosen by God,' he said –

JN: – 'for the destruction and the salvation of many in Israel,' yes.

SP: So how does it feel to be chosen to destroy people?

JN: Unless a kernel of wheat falls to the ground and dies, it remains a single seed.

SP: 'He will be a sign from God,' said Simeon, 'which many people will speak against and so reveal their secret thoughts.' So perhaps it was written in the stars that you would expose people, upset people. Probably not the child your mother hoped for.

JN: 'And sorrow, like a sharp sword, will break your own heart.'

SP: That's how Simeon ends, yes. And sorrow did break

your mother's heart, which we'll get to. But for now I'm just wondering why? Why this had to be, why you had to upset so many people, why so much had to be smashed and uprooted?

JN: Unless you turn and become as a little child –

SP: Here's my understanding of it, teacher: sometimes, when something is known by us, it's better if it becomes unknown, that we might know it again, know it afresh. Is that what you're saying? Sometimes we're so familiar with things – like our religious beliefs – that they congeal, lose their capacity to move us, and we need to start again, discover them again. And this is perhaps how you feel about the Torah, the Jewish law? That Israel has forgotten what it means?

JN: People justify themselves in the sight of men, but God knows their hearts.

SP: That's what I'm saying. You're taking things back to the inner life, back to people's hearts, which is where laws come from originally.

JN: The law and the prophets were until John.

SP: The laws and the prophets define the nation of Israel. But you're saying they've served their purpose?

JN: After John, the good news of the kingdom of God is preached and everyone is forcing their way into it.

SP: So the old religious laws are no longer important?

JN: Not at all.

21

s p: That's what you appear to be saying.

j n: No, it is easier for heaven and earth to pass away, than for even the tiniest point of the law to fall.

s p: You speak there as a good Rabbi should; you are a son of the synagogue after all. Yet the fact is, though, you challenge the law; and you challenge the Pharisees who are the upholders of the law, at some of their most sensitive points – like the keeping of the Sabbath, for instance.

j n: The Pharisees and the Scribes have received the keys of knowledge, but they have hidden them.

s p: Their religion obscures the truth?

j n: They do not go inside themselves yet they bar others from going in also!

s p: It's not a happy situation when the religious leaders are themselves blocking the doorway of understanding. But I suspect they're not the first, and won't be the last.

j n: The chief priests and the elders of the people came to me as I was teaching, and said, 'By what authority do you do these things? Who gave you this authority?'

s p: People do say you speak with authority.

j n: I said, 'I also will ask you one question, and if you answer that, then I will tell you by what authority I do these things.'

s p: So what was your question to them?

J N: 'The baptism John offered,' I said – 'what were its origins? Was it from heaven or from men?'

S P: So how did they respond?

J N: They debated among themselves!

S P: That was a clever question, teacher, and I can hear the debate from here: 'If we say John's baptism came from heaven,' they'll be saying, 'then Jesus will ask us, "Why then did you not believe him?"'

J N: 'But if we say, "It came from men," then what will the crowd do, because they all regard John as a prophet.'

S P: They were caught on the horns of a dilemma. So how did they answer in the end?

J N: They said: 'We don't know.'

S P: 'We don't know'? Well, I think you won that round in the arena.

J N: So I said to them, 'Then neither do I know by what authority I do these things!'

S P: Your treatment of the Sabbath was getting under their skin, of course. Like good Israelites, they kept the Sabbath law, as the Torah demands, unlike you and your followers, who, I'm told, plucked and crushed grain on the day of rest.

J N: Some of the Pharisees said to us, 'Why do you do that which is unlawful to do on the Sabbath day?'

SP: And it's a fair point, given the law. There are 39 forbidden actions on the Sabbath and 'harvesting' is one of them. Plucking grain would definitely come under 'harvesting', even I can see that.

JN: These people, they set aside the commandment of God and cling to the tradition of men.

SP: But this is the commandment of God, surely? Aren't the scriptures the commandment of God and the scriptures support the Sabbath laws!

JN: Haven't you read what David did when he was hungry?

SP: Remind me.

JN: How he and those with him entered the house of God and how David both took and ate the show bread.

SP: What's that?

JN: The bread meant for priests alone. He took it and then shared it with those who were with him.

SP: So what are you saying? That human need is the greatest law of all, even with the most holy things? And that the Sabbath is offered to us as a friend, rather than imposed on us as a tyrant?

JN: The Sabbath is made for man, not man for the Sabbath.

SP: That's well put, very memorable, but you must be aware how threatening this is to everyone. After all, keeping the Sabbath is the most distinctive of Jewish customs, the bedrock of their identity, a clear mark of separation between them and other cultures.

JN: A grapevine planted away from the father has no life. It will be torn up by its roots and perish.

SP: Even Hillel says that whoever has acquired the words of the law has acquired the life to come. But perhaps you feel we miss the point if we over-emphasize the law? Can rules only take us so far?

JN: The Sabbath is made for man.

SP: It's like the temple, if I understand you aright. If you look at the temple – and it's hard not to in Jerusalem – it appears to be made of bricks, and in one way it is. It's an important place. But more important than the bricks and the visible place is the identity and space inside, that's what you're saying. It's the quality of the space *inside* the temple that matters, for there lies its true identity. And it's the same with humans. It's the quality of space inside us that matters. But we find it easier to talk about external and less important things like the bricks or laws.

JN: Those who have ears, let them hear.

SP: Yet we can't get away from the fact that the Jewish law is part of their nationhood. In the past, Jewish fugitives have allowed themselves to be massacred rather than fight on the Sabbath. How do you feel about threatening someone's sense of identity?

JN: So tell me, is it lawful to do good or harm on the Sabbath?

SP: I know you've healed people on the holy day, which was controversial.

JN: And is it lawful to save someone or to kill someone on the Sabbath?

SP: When put like that, you make an ass of the law, but talk like this makes you enemies. Hillel would have supported your interpretation, but the Shammaites will not.

JN: Or again, what sheep-owner is there who, if his sheep falls into a pit on the Sabbath, will not take hold of it and lift it out?

SP: I understand.

JN: And how much more valuable is a man than a sheep!

SP: Really, I do understand.

JN: Therefore you also understand that it is lawful to do good on the Sabbath day.

SP: I do. But let's be honest, it's not just your views on the Sabbath, teacher. These religious leaders whom you clash with endlessly –

JN: – they're whitewashed tombs!

SP: Whitewashed tombs – impressive on the outside, but rotting within? Well, maybe, but they think your own lifestyle is rotten. They say you go to dubious parties, the like of which they'd never dream of attending.

JN: Can the wedding guests fast while the bridegroom is with them?

SP: Unlike John, your piety is not built around ascetic rigour.

JN: They're like children who sit in the marketplace and call one to another, saying, 'We piped to you and you didn't dance. We mourned and you didn't weep.'

SP: How do you mean?

JN: John the Baptizer comes neither eating bread nor drinking wine and they say, 'Ah, he must be mad!'

SP: That's true; that was their assessment.

JN: Then the son of man comes eating and drinking, and they say, 'Behold, a glutton and a drunkard.'

SP: Fair point. They can't have it both ways?

JN: 'Oh and he's a friend of tax collectors and sinners!' they say.

SP: Yes, that's an accusation I hear a lot; they really don't like the company you keep.

JN: Yet I tell you with certainty that the tax collectors and prostitutes are entering into the kingdom of God before them.

SP: Prostitutes ahead of the religious leaders? I'm warming to this kingdom.

JN: These leaders create heavy burdens that are difficult to carry, lay them on people's shoulders, and yet refuse to lift a finger to help them.

SP: They do good works, though, teacher. Many people have seen their good works.

JN: Precisely. All their works they do to be seen by many people.

SP: I hadn't thought of that. I suppose the robes do make their charitable acts rather public. The strange thing is, though, you're similar to the Pharisees in so many ways. Indeed, many Pharisees I talk to agree with you most of the time. But unlike some of them, you practise what you preach; or rather, you *are* what you preach, I think that may be it. There's no dissonance between word and action.

JN: These men – they make their phylacteries obvious, enlarge the fringes of their garments, love the place of honour at feasts, the best seats in the synagogues, the greetings in the marketplace – oh, and to be called 'Rabbi, Rabbi' by men.

SP: Everyone likes a label of status or affirmation.

JN: And they have a clever way of rejecting God's law in order to uphold their own.

SP: Give me an example.

JN: Moses commanded 'respect your father and mother.'

SP: True.

JN: But they teach that if someone has something that could

benefit their father or mother, but says, 'This belongs to God', then he is excused helping his mother and father!

SP: I see.

JN: In this way, the teaching they pass on cancels out the word of God.

SP: And yet for some reason, you can't reach them, teacher; you can't reach these supposedly holy people. You rail against them, but can't reach them. Are they too well-defended?

JN: When you bring forth what is within you, then that will save you; if you do not, then that will kill you.

SP: You mean they hide their true selves, which could save them, behind religious barriers which will kill them?

JN: A man cannot ride two horses or bend two bows.

SP: You cannot ride the horse of truth if you ride the horse of lies?

JN: But I will overturn this house –

SP: – the temple? –

JN: – I will overturn this house and none will be able to rebuild it.

SP: Dangerous words, teacher; no, worse, blasphemous words. The temple is God's house and the centre of the Jewish faith.

JN: It is a house of prayer.

SP: I can see what Josephus means. He told me that you Galileans are 'bellicose from infancy', that was his phrase. And John the Baptizer started the rot by declaring that God could make children of Abraham from stones! That really got their goat – the idea that to be one of God's people didn't depend on your family tree.

JN: John came to these men in the goodness of God.

SP: Well-disguised goodness.

JN: Yet they didn't believe him.

SP: Some did.

JN: Oh yes, the tax collectors and the prostitutes believed him!

SP: There's something visceral in the stand-off between you and organized religion, teacher; as if two worlds are at war; no, as if two ways of *being* are at war.

JN: Perhaps men think that I am come to bring peace to the world?

SP: There's more peace in your little finger than there was in the whole of John.

JN: Really? Yet I come to cast divisions upon the earth, with fire, sword, and war.

SP: That's what your words are like, teacher, a perfect description; they're a fire, a sword, and a war in the soul. No one escapes; they wound everyone. Yet these words are repelled with ferocity by your opponents.

JN: Do not give sacred things to dogs, for they may treat them as dung.

SP: People ignore or ridicule those who are beyond themselves or bigger than themselves. There's a fear of them, I suppose.

JN: And so do not throw pearls to swine, for they may treat them as waste.

SP: It appears to me that religion – and I've seen a lot – either makes people more human or less human. But is this what you expected? Did you expect it all to be so hard?

JN: I came to set the world on fire – but how I wish it were already kindled.

SP: You feel as though you're starting from scratch? Yet even a bellicose Galilean must appreciate the upset you cause. How disturbing it must be to be told that what you've always thought is holy, turns out not to be holy at all! A message like that could turn a lot of people violent.

JN: Understand the time.

SP: You're offering a fresh start, you mean. Yet I'm thinking of the Genesis story, when Lot, to save his life, has to leave his hometown of Sodom. He knows he must do it but still finds it very hard. It may have been a terrible city, but it was all he knew, and it's hard to leave what we know.

JN: If anyone desires to come after me, let him deny himself, take up his cross, and follow me.

SP: But they don't want to follow you. Why would they? The

Jewish community here in Palestine is more a synagogue than a state. It's the Law of Moses that counts in civil, religious, and personal matters. It's an edifice, and you're trying to pull it down.

JN: How right Isaiah was when he prophesied about them. 'These people,' says God, 'honour me with their words but their heart is really far from me. It is no use for them to worship me, for they teach man-made rules as though they were God's rules.'

SP: It's all they know, teacher; it's the dye they've been soaked in since birth. It's how they imagine themselves saved.

JN: Yes, and whoever desires to save his life will lose it, yet whoever will lose his life for my sake will find it.

SP: So like Lot, we are asked to leave our hometown, the town of our conditioning?

JN: Well, what does it profit a man if he gains the whole world and forfeits his life?

SP: You ask us to risk everything on the possibility there's some life beyond the one we know; a life beyond our familiar routine of attitude and belief. It's almost as if there's another self inside us, through a narrow gate, waiting to be discovered.

JN: So enter in by the narrow gate.

SP: Become naked to all I know?

JN: Wide is the gate and broad is the way that leads to destruction and many are those who enter in by it.

SP: They go with the flow like dead dogs in a stream?

JN: How narrow is the gate and restricted the way that leads to life, my friend. Few are those who find it. But –

SP: – but what?

JN: Seek and you shall discover.

SP: Seek and I'll discover?

JN: Seek and you shall discover.

SP: That is your passion, teacher, I sense that: the passion to loosen us from our old selves, from old ways, from our borrowed assumptions – that we might discover realities and truths perhaps obscured by daily life.

JN: Knock and the door shall be opened.

SP: Again, yes, but tell me – what about those who don't want to go inside? What about those who don't wish to be loosened from old ways? These words then become a death sentence. Folk hear them, seethe inside and, like water in a fire, they hiss against you. Is it hard being rejected?

JN: A man goes out to sow corn.

SP: Is this one of your stories?

JN: And as he scatters the seed in the field, some of it falls along the path and the birds come and eat it.

SP: Common enough.

JN: Some of it falls on rocky ground, where there's little soil.

SP: And it dies?

JN: No, the seed sprouts, because the soil isn't deep. But when the sun comes up, it burns the young shoots and because there's no depth for the roots, the plants die.

SP: Shame.

JN: And then some of the seed falls among thorn bushes, which grow up and choke the plants.

SP: And they don't produce corn?

JN: They produce no corn, no. But other seeds fall in good soil, and the plants sprout there, grow and produce much corn: some with thirty grains, some sixty, some with one hundred.

SP: A happy ending, teacher, but a story rooted in realism; a tragic story in a way about the soil of the human heart. Where the soil's good, there's growth, but where the soil's poor, nothing placed in it can grow. I can see why they hate you. And were I to follow you, they would hate me.

JN: So be happy when people hate you.

SP: That's just what the Essenes say. They would 'rather be among the persecuted than the persecutors, rather be among the hated than the haters; rather be among the scoffed-at than the scoffers.'

JN: If the light in you is darkness, how very dark it becomes.

sp: That's quite a thought, teacher. And as we talk, you put me in mind of an eastern sutra, which says this: 'Do good things, not for your own sake, but for all the beings in the universe. Save and liberate everyone you encounter, help them attain the wisdom of the way.' And you are such a man; this is what you do. But the awakening you wish for has been a mixed success at best. Some people have got it, while others, well, they've missed it completely. I mean, even your followers, whom you've spent time with, vary a great deal in their understanding.

jn: They are no more intelligent than the others.

sp: And doesn't that concern you?

jn: Be happy when people reject you, insult you, and say that you are evil.

sp: I mean, some got it for some of the time, and missed it for the rest; some half-woke, some stayed soundly asleep –

jn: – and dance for joy, because a great reward is kept for you in heaven.

sp: So you say. But to repeat myself: don't you wish things had been easier? Not even your family believed you.

jn: Who is my family?

sp: Well, that's what I wanted to talk about next.

THREE

Whatever happened to family values?

Jesus is from artisan stock and his family setting is the world of small farmers and independent craftsmen. He isn't one of the rich, but neither is he one of the poor. If he has embraced poverty, this has been his choice, voluntary suffering.

And though we now sit in a busy Jerusalem market, Jesus is still a country boy at heart. It's well-known that when preaching in Galilee, he didn't visit the larger towns such as Sepphoris, Gabara, or Tiberius. Jesus of Nazareth was both a son of his parents and the Galilean countryside.

SP: The temple incident, when you were twelve. I expect your mother has reminded you about it a few times. She's certainly reminded everyone else! She tells the story with some pride though I suspect it wasn't like that at the time.

JN: When I was twelve years old, we went up to Jerusalem according to the custom of the feast.

SP: Everyone had to go there for the three major festivals each year.

JN: Yes, and when were returning, I stayed behind here in Jerusalem.

SP: You were twelve and you stayed behind?

JN: My father and mother didn't realize and imagining I was somewhere in the travelling party, travelled a day's journey before asking for me among friends and relatives.

SP: Panic growing, I'd imagine.

JN: When they didn't find me, they returned to Jerusalem, and after three days found me in the temple, sitting with the teachers, both listening to them and asking questions.

SP: I suspect you were always bright, Jesus, even then. And that's why you give the Pharisees and Scribes such a hard time today. You know what they know, but then you know more.

JN: When they saw me in the temple, my mother and father were astonished, and my mother said, 'Son, why have you treated us this way? Your father and I have been worried out of our minds looking for you!'

SP: A natural reaction. So what did you say?

JN: Why have you been looking for me?

SP: That's what you said?

JN: Didn't you know that I must be in my father's house?

SP: A harsh response to your parents, teacher. But they took you home to Nazareth, with your mother wondering what kind of a son she had on her hands, and your father? Well, presumably he taught you carpentry and the building trade. You must have learned a lot from him.

JN: A son can do nothing on his own account, but only what he sees his father doing.

SP: Like father, like son.

JN: What the father does, the son copies.

SP: He was a good teacher?

JN: The father loves the son and shows him everything, all the secrets of his craft.

SP: And unsurprisingly, your stories are full of images taken from the building trade: the speck of sawdust in the eye; the dodgy builders skimping on foundations; oh, and the importance of drawing up a proper estimate before work begins!

JN: Well, would anyone think of building a tower without first sitting down and calculating the cost, to see whether he can afford to finish it?

SP: Only a fool.

JN: Because if he does, when he's laid a foundation and then clearly can't finish, everyone will to mock him. 'This man began the job,' they'll say, 'but wasn't able to finish!'

SP: You do get builders like that, but staying with your family, you have four brothers, of course – James, Judas, Joseph, and Simon, and several sisters. But – and this isn't easy to say – things started to turn a little sour between you all. We all want happy families but that isn't how it was for you. They didn't understand you, perhaps? And if the truth be told, you began to separate yourself from them. Your brothers, for instance: they say you deceived them over the Feast of Shelters. They wanted you to go with them to Jerusalem but you refused.

JN: I said the right time for me has not yet come.

s p: You told them you were going to stay in Galilee.

j n: You go to the festival, I said, but I am not going.

s p: And yet you did go, teacher, you did go. After your brothers had left, you went to the festival in secret, which some might see as devious. And John also told me about the incident at the wedding in Cana.

j n: My mother was there, as was I with my followers. The wine runs out and my mother turns to me and says, 'They have no wine left.'

s p: That's unfortunate at a wedding. So what did you do?

j n: I said, 'Woman, what have I to do with you?'

s p: 'What have I to do with you?' She's your mother and you say that? It's like the temple story, only ruder still, for you're no longer a precocious youth but an adult. Had you perhaps reached a new stage in your life, when you said goodbye to conventional human ties? John is clear about your brothers' lack of support. In fact, word is that people were saying 'He's gone mad' and that your family set out to take charge of you.

j n: It's true that while I was speaking to a crowd of people, one of those there told me that my mother and brothers were waiting outside to speak with me.

s p: So presumably you went to see them?

j n: No.

s p: No?

JN: No. I said to him, 'Who is my mother? Who are my brothers?'

SP: That's a shocking question for a good Jewish boy to ask.

JN: I pointed towards my followers, and said, 'Here are my mother and my brothers!'

SP: You said that?

JN: Here are my mother and brothers! For whoever does the will of my father who is in heaven, he is my brother and sister and mother.

SP: So you're redefining family values; quite a challenge. The family is an important social structure, but you're saying there's something more important. From here on, blood loyalty and clan are secondary to commitment to the kingdom of God?

JN: So listen –

SP: – I'm all ears.

JN: When you arrange a dinner or a supper, don't call your friends or your brothers or your relatives or your rich neighbours.

SP: Why not?

JN: Because they might return the favour and pay you back.

SP: But that's the idea, isn't it?

JN: No, when you make a feast, ask the poor, the maimed, the lame, or the blind; and you will be blessed because they don't have the resources to repay you.

SP: You don't make it easy, do you? The thing is, friends and family are a security for us; but you're saying that we must love without boundaries.

JN: And believe me when I say that whoever cannot free themselves from their father and their mother cannot be my follower.

SP: Really?

JN: And whoever cannot free themselves from their brother and their sister and does not bear their cross as I do – well, they shall not be worthy of me either.

SP: You're swimming against the tide, teacher, but I think I see what you're saying. Our families take us back to our old conditioning, to the judgements and customs which formed us and therefore away from our original selves.

JN: One of my followers said, 'I will follow – but allow me first to bury my father.'

SP: Fair enough.

JN: I said, follow me and leave the dead to bury their own dead.

SP: And the 5th commandment – the one that enjoins us to respect our father and mother?

JN: When a blind person leads another blind person, they both fall into a pit.

SP: We must acquire lives of our own?

FOUR

Is it all in the preparation?

*From what I can gather, Jesus left his family home and trade with
the arrival on the scene of John the Baptizer; and his baptism by
John in the river Jordan proved a turning point in his life. It's
said that he had a profound spiritual experience by the river, in
which the heavens appeared to be torn wide open with the spirit
of God descending on him like a dove. It all reminds me of the
Old Testament story of Jacob's ladder. Jacob is asleep in the desert
and dreams of a ladder coming down from heaven, with angels
walking up and down. Here are two worlds brought together,
heaven and earth; and certainly from this time on, Jesus never
looked back. From this experience of light, he walked into the
darkness.*

*But how had he prepared for what was to come? I wished to go
back to the early days of his calling.*

SP: Was it all in the preparation, teacher?

JN: It is not possible for anyone to go into the strong man's
house and take it by force, unless he first binds the strong
man's hands; then he will plunder his house.

SP: And did you perhaps need to test your strength in some
way?

JN: Yes, the kingdom of the father is like someone who wants
to kill a great man. First, he draws the sword in his own house
and drives it into the wall.

SP: He's practising?

JN: That he might know his hand will be strong, yes.

SP: And once he knows?

JN: Then he slays the great man.

SP: So after your baptism by John, like a carpenter testing his wood, you set off into the wilderness to test yourself.

JN: If you don't fast from the world, you will not find the kingdom.

SP: And so you withdrew from the world, including all food, because you didn't eat for forty days.

JN: Blessed are those who hunger, for they will be filled.

SP: There's a lovely old pharisaic saying: 'The world is an ante-chamber for the future one; prepare yourself well in the ante-chamber that you may appear properly in the reception room.' And you chose the desert to prepare, reckoned by many to be the habitat of demons. And it was after forty days without food that you faced the arch-demon.

JN: The devil said to me, 'If you are the Son of God, command this stone to become bread.'

SP: You were hungry; that must have been tempting.

JN: I said, 'It is written, "Man cannot live on bread alone."'

SP: He needs inner resources; you would say he needs God.

JN: The devil then led me up a high mountain and showed me

all the kingdoms of the world in a moment of time.

SP: They were spread out before you in a vision?

JN: He said, 'I will give you all this power and all this wealth for it is mine to give to whoever I choose.'

SP: A bit brazen.

JN: 'And it will all be yours, Jesus, if only you bow down to me.'

SP: We can see his needs clear enough, but I don't suppose you colluded with his cravings.

JN: I said, 'Get behind me Satan! For it is written, "You shall worship the Lord your God and him only shall you serve."'

SP: That reminds me of something from the *Dhammapada*: 'Better than all the happiness on earth or in heaven, greater than dominion over all the worlds, is the first step in the Noble Path.' And your noble path began here.

JN: He then led me to Jerusalem, and set me on the pinnacle of the temple, and said, 'If you are the Son of God, cast yourself down from here, for it is written, "He will give his angels to you as guardians," and also, "Their hands will carry you, lest perhaps you dash your foot against a stone."'

SP: So now you've got the devil quoting scripture at you, which is a bit unnerving.

JN: I said to him, 'It has also been written, "You shall not tempt the Lord your God."'

SP: Which presumably went down like a vat of cold vomit?

JN: And then when he'd completed his temptations, he departed from me – until another time.

SP: Yes, he always comes back, doesn't he? But did you see things differently after that?

JN: I saw Satan falling like lightning from heaven.

SP: Really? That must have been rather fine! But were you anxious nevertheless; anxious about the unknown, about what might lie ahead for you? It does seem to me that from here on, you started on a journey into the heart of darkness.

JN: Don't be anxious for tomorrow.

SP: This is your motto?

JN: Don't be anxious for tomorrow, but let tomorrow be anxious for itself. Each day's challenges are sufficient.

SP: That's a wise saying. We must learn to laugh at our anxieties, as you say. And so you returned to Galilee, and began to preach in the local synagogues, including your hometown of Nazareth. That must have been interesting.

JN: I stood up to read the scriptures, and was handed the Book of Isaiah.

SP: One of the great prophets of Israel.

JN: I unrolled the scroll and found the place where it is written, 'The spirit of the lord is upon me, because he has chosen me to bring good news to the poor.'

SP: This was the reading you chose?

JN: 'He has sent me to proclaim liberty to the captives and recovery of sight to the blind; to set free the oppressed and announce the time has come when the Lord will set free his people.'

SP: An ambitious calling.

JN: I rolled up the scroll, gave it back to the attendant, and sat down.

SP: The drama was over.

JN: And then I said, 'Today, this scripture came true, even as you heard it being read.'

SP: The drama wasn't over! You really said that?

JN: Today, this scripture came true, even as you heard it being read.

SP: Quite a moment in your life, I'd imagine. So the time for preparation was done. This was the real thing.

JN: 'Isn't he the son of Joseph?' they said.

SP: This was your hometown. They'd seen you grow up and knew you well. You were just Joseph's boy. No one's a messiah to the one who taught him to walk.

JN: You will no doubt quote me the proverb, 'Doctor, heal

yourself'.

SP: Or perhaps 'A doctor for others but himself full of sores,' as Euripides wrote in one of his plays. Was this cynicism the reason you now left Nazareth?

JN: I was not able to perform any miracles there, apart from placing my hands on a few sick people.

SP: Were you surprised at the people's lack of faith?

JN: I was greatly surprised.

FIVE

What makes a good prayer?

Jesus took part in synagogue worship, which used formal prayers;
but apparently also went off to be alone in the mountains and
desert. He'd disappear early, before the demands of the day. So I
was eager to know: what makes a good prayer?

SP: You recently lost your temper.

JN: Don't judge, and you won't be judged.

SP: It wasn't meant to be a judgement; but then again, perhaps
it was.

JN: With whatever judgement you judge, you will be judged,
and with whatever measure you measure, it will be measured
to you.

SP: I understand. But what interests me most is the cause of
your rage. You went into the temple here in Jerusalem, saw
people buying and selling things, and assaulted them with
both word and whip.

JN: 'My house shall be called a house of prayer,' I said, 'but
you have made it a den of robbers!'

SP: So you flung over the moneylenders' tables and kicked
over the chairs of the dove-sellers. And how very similar your
words were to those of the prophet Jeremiah! Centuries before
he, too, had stood in the temple, and said, 'Do you think that
my temple is a hiding place for robbers? I will drive you out of
my sight as I drove out your relatives!'

JN: As I say, 'My house shall be called a house of prayer.'

SP: The temple had lost its identity as a place of prayer, and prayer matters to you, teacher. But then unlike most people, you have a profound trust in your heavenly father.

JN: See the birds of the sky who neither sow, reap, nor store food in barns. Yet your heavenly father feeds them. Aren't you of much more value than these birds?

SP: With such limitless trust prayer must be both easy and delightful.

JN: Or consider the lilies of the field and how they grow. They don't toil, they don't spin, yet I tell you that even Solomon in all his glory was not dressed like one of these.

SP: Your eyes are never far from creation, teacher. Indeed, I sometimes think it's your scripture even more than the scriptures themselves.

JN: And if God so clothes the grass of the field, which is here today but tomorrow is thrown in the fire, then how much more will you be dressed, you of little faith?

SP: We learn from what we see and hear, and I suppose some of us had bad teachers of prayer; people who replaced simple trust with something else like pomposity, fear, or self-righteousness.

JN: Two men went up into the temple to pray; one was a Pharisee and the other was a tax collector.

SP: Tax collectors know nothing about the prayer. I know you like to speak well of them but I've never met a nice one myself, and I've met many nice Pharisees.

JN: The Pharisee stood and prayed to himself like this: 'God, I thank you that I am not like the rest of men.'

SP: Not a good start, I grant you. We'll call him Proud Peter.

JN: 'I thank you that I am not like other men – extortioners, the unrighteous, adulterers, or even such low-life as this tax collector. I fast twice a week and give tithes of all that I receive.'

SP: It seems Proud Peter must feel superior to others to make himself feel good. He must always have a list of people *less* good than him.

JN: So then see the tax collector –

SP: – whom we'll just call Low-Life –

JN: – standing far away. He won't even lift up his eyes to heaven, but beats his breast, saying, 'God, be merciful to me, a sinner!'

SP: Which he is, because all those tax collectors are on the make.

JN: Do not condemn and you won't be condemned –

SP: – OK, OK –

JN: – yet I tell you, it was this man –

SP: – Low-Life? –

JN: – who went back to his house having made God smile, rather than the other; for everyone who exalts himself will be humbled but they who humble themselves will be exalted.

SP: Is that so? Then it's not so much the act of prayer which is important, but the attitude we bring to prayer. If we're full of ourselves, it's an empty experience. But when trust is there –

JN: – ask, and it will be given to you.

SP: You do keep things simple, teacher, even if it's simply impossible.

JN: Your father in heaven knows your needs.

SP: Maybe, but as you know, that doesn't stop a number of healers indulging in a few prayerful theatrics. They love all the 'abracadabra' stuff with their Jewish and pagan amulets.

JN: Do not use a lot of meaningless words, as the pagans do. They imagine that God will hear them merely because their prayers are so long.

SP: And it's not just words with these healers; it's much more theatrical than that. Young Tobit, for instance, burnt the heart and liver of a fish to keep the demon Asmodeus away from his bride. While the showman Eleazar, for his exorcisms, fills a bowl of water for the expelled demon to knock over on leaving – so the audience can see what's happening! But not you, teacher – you apparently give a single command to the demon to quit, or the leprosy to disappear, the withered hand to stretch out, the deaf ears to open or the storm to abate. Just a single command.

JN: 'When you pray, say this:

'Our father in heaven, may your name be held holy,
your kingdom come and your will be done on earth as it is
   in heaven.
Give us day by day our daily bread.
And forgive us our sins, as we ourselves forgive everyone
   who is indebted to us.
And bring us not into temptation, but deliver us from the
   evil one.

SP: And it's that simple?

JN: Your father in heaven knows your needs.

SP: It's the sort of simple prayer you could almost breathe throughout the day, and alongside trust I notice another important attitude there –

JN: – Forgive us our sins as we forgive everyone who is indebted to us?

SP: Yes, forgiving others is never easy.

JN: Peter once came to me and said, 'Master, how often should I forgive someone who hurts me?'

SP: Good question. I find once hard enough.

JN: 'Up to seven times?' he said.

SP: Seven times seems excessive.

JN: Not seven times, I said, but seventy times seven.

SP: Seventy times seven is a ridiculous amount of forgiveness.

JN: So hear this. You have heard in the past that people were told 'Do not commit murder'?

SP: Of course.

JN: But now I tell you that who ever is angry with his brother will be brought to trial.

SP: The courts will be busy.

JN: And whoever calls his brother a 'good-for-nothing' will be brought before the council, while anyone naming his brother a worthless fool will be in danger of the fires of hell.

SP: And quite unfit for prayer?

JN: Quite so. So if you're about to offer your gift to God at the altar and remember that someone has something against you, leave your gift there in front of the altar, go at once and make peace with them –

SP: – and *then* come back and offer your gift to God?

JN: And then come back and offer your gift to God, yes.

SP: I'm learning.

JN: So whenever you stand praying, if you hold anything against anyone –

s p: – anyone? –

j n: – yes, anyone, forgive them, so that your father in heaven may also forgive you your stumblings.

s p: And now you remind me of Rabbi Hanna, 'The commandment to love your neighbour is a commandment on which the whole world hangs,' he says, 'a mighty oath from Sinai. If you hate your neighbour whose deeds are wicked like your own, I the Lord will punish you as your judge. And if you love your neighbour whose deeds are like your own, I the Lord will be faithful to you and have mercy on you.' You and the rabbi both see our treatment by God as reflecting our treatment of others.

j n: True. Set free and you will be set free, and one more thing –

s p: Yes?

j n: Don't pray like the hypocrites.

s p: How do they pray?

j n: They love to stand up and pray in the houses of worship and on the street corners so that everyone will see them.

s p: They're quite hard to miss when in full flow.

j n: But when you pray, go to your room, close the door, and pray to your father who is unseen.

s p: As you do. Only you withdraw to the hills. Mark told me you went out long before daylight.

JN: Your father, who sees what you do in private, will reward you.

SP: So good prayer needs trust, a readiness to forgive others, and seclusion.

JN: Close the door, yes.

SP: And perhaps stillness of heart? You mentioned something about Martha.

JN: I remember Martha, the sister of Mary, once received me into her house. Mary was there, sitting listening to me, while Martha was much distracted by things to do.

SP: Some people do like to be busy; they find it hard simply to be.

JN: But then she came up to me and said 'Don't you care, sir, that my sister has left me to serve alone?'

SP: She wanted Mary to be busy as well.

JN: 'Ask her to help me!' she demanded.

SP: Sisters at war, or perhaps two ways of being at war.

JN: I said 'Martha, Martha, you are anxious and troubled about many things, but just the one thing is needed.'

SP: Just the one thing – do you mean the quiet listening?

JN: Mary had chosen well and that couldn't be taken away from her.

SP: I hadn't expected it, teacher, but in many ways, you teach quite a private religion; a religion of trust, forgiveness, seclusion, and stillness. Who knows, in time you might even put the high priests out of business!

JN: I reveal my mysteries to those who become worthy.

SP: This is how it is?

JN: Whoever seeks will discover; and whoever knocks from the inside, the door will open to them.

SIX

What makes a good person?

It's the arrival of some grapes and figs at our table that starts his trail of thought, though it wasn't the answer I expected.

SP: What makes someone good, teacher?

JN: They do not gather these grapes from thorn bushes.

SP: No.

JN: Nor do they pluck these figs from camel-thistles.

SP: Why would you?

JN: Such things do not bear fruit.

SP: So which of us do bear fruit, teacher? I mean, what makes a good person?

JN: The good person offers goodness to the world from the content of their heart; while the perverse person offers perversity from the content of their heart.

SP: So it's all about the heart?

JN: That which people reveal outwardly is the mere overflow of their heart, yes.

SP: So we are to have hearts of gold and all will be well. But how to acquire such a heart, I wonder?

JN: Whoever searches must continue to search until they find.

SP: We are never to give up on the search.

JN: And when you find, you will be disturbed.

SP: Well, that's very true. The search often brings us to disturbing places; we find things perhaps we didn't want to find. The temptation then is to give up or turn back.

JN: And being disturbed, you will marvel and will reign over all.

SP: So you describe a sequence, teacher: first quest, then discovery, then discomfort – and then wonder, joy, and a sense of exaltation. Have you seen such discovery in anyone?

JN: Hear this.

SP: A true story?

JN: I was passing through Jericho.

SP: I lived there for a while; I didn't like it much.

JN: There was a man named Zacchaeus. He was a high-ranking tax collector and he was rich.

SP: Well, he would be. I've never met a poor tax collector; certainly not in Jericho.

JN: He was trying to see who I was, but couldn't because of the crowd, being on the short side himself.

SP: I think I may know him.

JN: So he ran on ahead and climbed up into a sycamore tree so as to see me better as I passed.

SP: He was determined, I'll give him that.

JN: When I came to that place, I looked up and saw him there.

SP: Up the tree?

JN: And I said to him, 'Zacchaeus, hurry now and climb down, for today I'd like to visit your house.'

SP: His face must have been a picture!

JN: He was down in some haste and received me very joyfully.

SP: As well he might, but how did the crowd react to your new friendship?

JN: When they saw it, they all complained, saying, 'He has gone to the house of a sinner.'

SP: And Zacchaeus?

JN: Zacchaeus said to me, 'Lord, I'm going to give half my goods to the poor. And more, if I have wrongfully exacted anything of anyone, I will restore four times as much.'

SP: That would be a long queue of claimants. But I grant you, that's quite a change of heart.

JN: I said to him, 'Today, salvation has come to this house'.

SP: So salvation is looking at things in a new way, and I'm wondering how this happens? We can't change ourselves, we can't leave what we are, unless we have somewhere new to go to – and you offered Zacchaeus somewhere new, a different way of being in the world.

JN: The son of man comes to seek and to save that which is lost.

SP: Previously, Zacchaeus had only known what he knew, a sense of lack within himself, which he tried to calm through greed. But you offered a new way of seeing the world.

JN: The lamp of the body is the eye.

SP: And the eyes of Zacchaeus changed.

JN: When your eye is well, your whole body is full of light.

SP: That's true. And when it isn't well?

JN: When your eye is unwell, your whole body is full of darkness.

SP: They say the body is nine parts light and darkness, teacher, or perhaps a combination of the two.

JN: I have heard it said.

SP: So before he met you, Zacchaeus must have been seven parts dark and two parts light, but afterwards? Seven parts light surely? Maybe eight parts! All that light flooding through the dark areas!

JN: So see the light in you isn't darkness.

SP: Like Zacchaeus, we are to draw back the shutters on our lives?

JN: If your whole body is well lit, having no part dark, it will be full of light, as when the glowing lamp shines all around.

SP: And it starts with our eyes, with how we look at things.

JN: I was watching the rich people who were putting their gifts into the treasury.

SP: Ah yes, quite a sight. They do give generously, if rather obviously, to charity.

JN: I then saw a poor widow drop in two brass coins.

SP: Not everyone's so generous.

JN: No, truly I tell you, this poor widow put in more than all of them.

SP: More? She can't have put in more.

JN: The others, they gave to God from their fat abundance, but the widow, she gave from her thin poverty; she gave all she had to live on.

SP: There's a recklessness to such giving, teacher. And you like recklessness.

JN: So do not be anxious.

SP: Laugh in anxiety's face.

JN: Do not be anxious about where your food or drink will come from.

SP: You have no time for the anxious, teacher. You see anxiety as an act of fear or pride – a sign we're taking ourselves too seriously, perhaps, and God not seriously enough.

JN: Your food and drink – these are things the pagans are always concerned about.

SP: So we're back with trust, aren't we? Everything comes back to trust. They say all roads lead to Rome, but with you, they all lead to trust.

JN: So you can love your enemies.

SP: I beg your pardon?

JN: Love your enemies.

SP: Well, these are new words, teacher. Other rabbis tell us to love our neighbour, but you go further here. You demand our love be unconditional, including love for our enemies?

JN: Do good to those who hate you, yes.

SP: You know what your opponents say. They say that what is new in your teaching is not true. And what is true in your teaching is not new. But this sounds to me both new and true.

JN: Bless those who curse you, pray for those who mistreat you, love your enemies.

SP: Yet this requires such trust, teacher; a lake of trust within fed daily by freshwater. And I see problems. I'm thinking of those Galileans for instance, who Pilate had killed. Do you remember them? Everyone was talking about it. They were murdered while offering sacrifices to God. Did they not trust enough?

JN: Do you really think that because they were killed in that way they were worse sinners than other Galileans?

SP: It's what people say. And then there was that building which collapsed in Siloam, killing eighteen? What are we to make of news like that?

JN: Again, do you think that this proves that they were worse than all the other people living in Jerusalem?

SP: It's what people assume. 'They must have sinned,' they say.

JN: No, no, no – but unless you think again, readjust your ideas, you will die as they did.

SP: People have beliefs, teacher, but that's not the same as trust – is that what you're saying?

JN: Blessed is the one who has suffered.

SP: How so?

JN: Blessed is the one who has suffered; they have found life.

sp: You're saying suffering cracks belief, which is based on ideas, and replaces it with trust, which is rooted in relationship?

jn: And blessed are those who weep now, for they shall laugh.

sp: Hot tears melt discredited notions and water the ground for trust?

jn: As I say, do not be anxious –

sp: – for trust opens parts of our mind which other senses cannot reach? It's beginning to make sense, teacher. All belief has to be contorted and jerked to fit the facts, but trust just lives the moment, quite freely. And if someone can do that, just live the moment –

jn: – then they are like a house-builder, who digs deep into the ground, and lays a foundation on the rock.

sp: That's a good image.

jn: When the flood comes, the water smashes against that house, but cannot shake it, because it's founded on the rock.

sp: So please increase my trust.

jn: If you had trust the size of a mustard seed, you would tell a sycamore tree, 'Be uprooted, and be planted in the sea,' and it would obey you.

sp: You make things so simple and yet so hard; so attractive yet so impossible. What do you say to those who struggle?

JN: I say, 'Come to me, all you who labour and are weighed down by life, and I will give you rest.'

SP: That's a tantalizing promise. Your followers tell me that sometimes you were all so busy, that you didn't have time to eat; and that then, you'd take them off for a rest.

JN: I'd say, 'Let us go off by ourselves to some place where we'll be alone, and you can rest for a while.'

SP: Everyone needs rest.

JN: So take my yoke upon you, and learn from me, for I am gentle and lowly in heart; and you will find rest for your soul.

SP: And have you found rest for your soul, teacher? Your family think you're mad and the authorities harass you every step of the way. That's a heavy load to bear.

JN: No, my yoke is easy and my burden is light.

SP: I can never tell when you're joking.

SEVEN

What on earth is the kingdom of God?

*The real action for Jesus started after the arrest of John the
Baptizer. The preparation was over, and he travelled through
Galilee with the words: 'The time is come; the kingdom of God is
upon you.'*

*Galilee was the base for a threefold ministry. There was his broad
appeal to the public through synagogue addresses, preaching
in the open air, discussion and questions. Then there were the
healings I've heard so much about; and finally, the training of his
followers, which proved only a partial success.*

*John had raved at people, as prophets do. But messiahs must do
more than rave. They need to bring a vision of some sort, a dream;
and I'm wondering what dream Jesus brings? I'm told it's the
kingdom of God. But no one can quite tell me what it is.*

SP: We must talk about the kingdom, because I'm confused.
You say we must become like children.

JN: *(Pointing to a group of women feeding their young.)* Those
little ones over there, feeding at the breast.

SP: Yes?

JN: They are like those who enter into the kingdom.

SP: So if I become a child, or like a child, I shall enter the
kingdom?

JN: When you make the two one, and when you make the

67

inside as the outside, and the outside as the inside and the upper-side as the lower.

sp: Wait a minute, are you talking about bringing together different aspects of our lives?

jn: And when you make the male and the female into a single one, so that the male is not male and the female is not female, and when you have eyes in your eyes and a hand in your hand and a foot in your foot, and an image in your image, then yes, you shall enter the kingdom.

sp: You're saying that we shall enter the kingdom because, like a child, we are at one with all things inside ourselves and therefore outside ourselves?

jn: Appear neither naked nor clothed; neither sitting nor standing; neither laughing nor crying.

sp: These words continue the theme of oneness. You're saying we should not appear different to others in our outward expression, but always regard ourselves as part of the whole? I've heard such teaching from the East, teaching of our oneness with all things as a more true way; and with eyes such as these we will see, and with hands such as these we will both give and receive, and with such feet that we shall know the way?

jn: When you make the two one, yes.

sp: But still you don't define the kingdom. You say it's like this or it's like that but you won't say what it is, won't be pinned down.

JN: Listen.

SP: I'm listening.

JN: The disciples of John the Baptizer came to me.

SP: I did hear your behaviour worried him, but that was inevitable, because he was different to you. He saw the kingdom coming through abstinence, through violence against his body, and that wasn't really your way. So what message did his followers bring?

JN: 'John the Baptizer sent us to ask if you are the one he says is going to come, or whether we should be expecting someone else?'

SP: And your reply?

JN: 'Go back and tell John what you have seen and heard,' I said. 'The blind can see, the lame can walk, victims of the dreaded skin disease are declared clean, the deaf can hear, the dead are raised, and good news is preached to the poor!'

SP: 'The kingdom of God is at hand!' as John himself preached. But perhaps he was surprised by how it looked in your hands. You've surprised other people as well, of course, with your talk of the kingdom. One rabbi calls you 'an unoriginal Pharisee who gets too excited about the coming of the kingdom, and identifies himself with it far too much.'

JN: He who is near to me is near to the fire.

SP: That's your understanding?

JN: And he who is far from me is far from the kingdom. So now imagine being invited to a marriage feast.

SP: A marriage feast?

JN: Yes.

SP: I don't get invited to a lot of weddings now. I used to, when I was younger, of course.

JN: But if you do –

SP: – if I do –

JN: – don't sit in the best seat, since perhaps someone more honourable than you might be invited.

SP: I think there's a fair chance of that.

JN: And then, of course, the one who invited you would have to come and ask you to give up your seat for them.

SP: Embarrassing.

JN: So go and sit in the lowest place.

SP: Allow self-importance to dissolve.

JN: So that when your host sees you there, he may say 'Friend, move up higher!'

SP: Ah, a pleasant surprise indeed!

JN: And then you'll be honoured by all who sit at the table

with you. For everyone who exalts himself will be humbled and whoever humbles himself will be exalted.

SP: This is all rather unusual, teacher. It's a strange kingdom you describe and I have to say, an inner work of some challenge. A misguided self-importance is the cornerstone of our lives for most of the time. But whatever it may or may not be, this kingdom *seems* to be your code word for the ultimate good.

JN: The blind can see, the lame can walk –

SP: – it's a big salvation, a big healing, a big *homecoming* in a way.

JN: There was a man who had two sons.

SP: Is this a story of the kingdom?

JN: The younger one said to his father, 'Give me the share of property that is coming to me.'

SP: That seems a bit pushy.

JN: So the father divides up the property, and not long after, the younger son takes his share and goes off to a faraway country where he squanders his possessions in rather reckless living.

SP: He struggled with the idea of delayed gratification; he just couldn't wait.

JN: And then when he has spent all he had, a famine hits the country, leaving him in serious need.

SP: Oh dear.

JN: In the end, he hires himself out to a farmer who employs him to feed the pigs. But he's so hungry, even the pig food is tempting, because no one is giving him anything.

SP: Dire straits indeed.

JN: And then he comes to himself.

SP: A light goes on inside?

JN: 'How many of my father's hired hands have enough bread,' he says, 'yet here I am, dying of hunger. I'll get up off my knees, return to him and say: "Father, I have fallen short before heaven and before you, and I'm no longer worthy to be called your son. Treat me as one of your hired hands."'

SP: That was his plan.

JN: Yes, so he gets up and sets off for home –

SP: – embarrassing –

JN: – and yet, while he's still far away, his father sees him and, filled with compassion, runs towards him and embraces him and kisses him.

SP: That must have been a bit of a surprise for the son!

JN: The young man explains that he has fallen short before heaven and before his father and that he is no longer worthy to be called his son.

SP: Which is true in a way.

JN: But the father says to his servants, 'Quickly, find the best robe available and put it on him with a ring on his finger and shoes on his feet. And then bring the fattened calf and kill it, and let us eat and celebrate. For this my son was dead and is alive again; he was lost and is found!'

SP: The kingdom of God is a homecoming, when like the hungry son, we wake up, or as you say, come to ourselves?

JN: You become like the wise fisherman who cast his net into the sea and drew from the depths a catch of many small fish.

SP: Small fish are a bit of a waste of time.

JN: But among them, the wise fisherman found a large fish.

SP: Ah! So what did he do?

JN: Without hesitation, he decided to keep the large fish but throw all the small fish back into the sea.

SP: So let me understand – we are to seek the kingdom and that alone, ignoring all else? As Socrates said, 'There's so much I have no need of.' And just to be clear about this – the kingdom of God is not a place but a state; a state of being? The state of the hungry son, for instance, who suddenly 'came to himself' whilst feeding the pigs.

JN: If those who guide say the kingdom of God is in the sky –

SP: – and there are a few of those! –

JN: – then the birds are closer than you. And if they say, 'Look, it is there in the sea!' then the fish are already there.

SP: So where is it?

JN: The kingdom is both inside you and outside you.

SP: I suppose we're rather literal people. We like a time and a place for everything, and all things boxed and sorted. When is it and where is it? We demand a beginning and an end, a venue and a ticket. But I sense the kingdom is more elusive than that, like a scent on the breeze, coming and going.

JN: The kingdom of the father is spread out upon the earth and people do not see it.

SP: Is that so? And if it is, why is it so? I mean, why do we not recognize it? Are we perhaps blinded by our past, and looking for the wrong things? You're saying something new is at hand.

JN: No one puts a piece of unshrunk cloth on an old garment.

SP: Definitely not.

JN: For the patch tears away from the garment and a worse hole is made.

SP: I think you've put your finger on it there. That's why you cause such consternation! Because that's exactly what you're doing: you're tearing people up inside as the new fights with the old!

JN: And neither do people put new wine into old wineskins, or else the skins will split, the wine will spill, and the skins ruined. No, they put new wine into fresh wineskins and both are preserved.

SP: According to Mary Magdalene, you've come to help free us from the ignorance that is attachment or corruption. You yourself are the embodiment of the kingdom, she says; the embodiment of the practice of good.

JN: Why do you call me good?

SP: It was just what Mary was saying.

JN: No one is good but God alone.

SP: I'll remember that: not even Jesus is good, and good sits alongside evil in each of our hearts, health and ill-health side by side. We are speckled people.

JN: Listen. The kingdom of God is like the farmer who has some fine seed.

SP: OK.

JN: But his enemy comes at night and sows weed among his good seed.

SP: So now everything's mixed up, which is what I was saying; we're speckled. Presumably the farmer then tries to root out the weeds?

JN: No, he doesn't allow his workers to pull them up.

SP: Why not?

JN: He fears they might pull up the wheat as well.

SP: Which they might.

JN: But come the harvest, the weeds will be obvious enough, he says, and then they will be pulled up and burned.

SP: So in a way, things are coming to a head. The prophets of old said the kingdom was in the future; John the Baptizer said the kingdom was at hand; but you, Jesus, you say it's within us, in the midst of us, here, now.

JN: There are some standing here who will not taste death before they see the son of man come with power.

SP: Really?

EIGHT

What hurts people?

SP: I wonder why it is we struggle to learn new things. Is it because the only way to learn something new is to abandon something old?

JN: A rich man was granted a big harvest.

SP: You do love stories.

JN: And the rich man thought to himself, 'What will I do now, because I don't have room to store my crops?'

SP: Let me think – he gave them away to the poor?

JN: No, he said, 'This is what I will do. I'll pull down my barns and build bigger ones and there, in my new huge barns, I will store all my grain and my goods!'

SP: Ah.

JN: Yes, and I will tell my soul, 'You lucky man! Here you are with a great many goods piled high for many years ahead. Take your ease, eat, drink, and be merry!'

SP: While the world looks on in envy.

JN: But God said to him, 'You fool! Tonight your soul is required of you. And then what future is there for all your supposed riches?'

SP: Ouch!

JN: And that is the way for those who are rich in possessions but poor towards God.

SP: In my experience, most of the rich imagine they've got there by their own hard work. They have a mindset of entitlement.

JN: Woe to those who are rich; they have received their consolation.

SP: Not that you meet them too often, I'd imagine.

JN: No, I once met a rich young man. 'What must I do to gain eternal life?' he asked.

SP: He wanted it all.

JN: 'You know the commandments', I said. 'Do not commit murder, do not commit adultery, do not steal, do not accuse anyone falsely, do not cheat, respect your father and mother.'

SP: And his response?

JN: 'Ever since I was young I have obeyed these!' he said.

SP: Rich and good.

JN: 'Then go and sell all you have and give the money to the poor,' I said, 'and you will have riches in heaven.'

SP: And so you left him happy?

JN: No, he went away sad.

SP: And the man with his barns is a sad story, too. He can't learn something new because he can't let go of something old. Unable to abandon his anxieties about survival – hence all the barn-building and barn-filling – he's also unable to discover a new way of living. But tell me: are possessions really such a problem for us?

JN: Someone once said to me, 'Teacher, tell my brother to divide the inheritance with me.'

SP: Inheritance arguments are the worst.

JN: I said to him, 'Man, just who made me a judge or a divider over you? Beware! Keep yourselves from covetousness, for a man's life does not consist in the number of things he possesses.'

SP: So what are we to do?

JN: As I say, sell that which you have and give gifts to the needy.

SP: I see.

JN: Make for yourself a purse which doesn't wear out, a treasure in the heavens that doesn't rust, where no thief can reach and no moth can destroy.

SP: It's true a burglar wouldn't get much from you – apart from some worn-out sandals.

JN: Where your treasure is, there will your heart be also.

SP: Is it simply that even the best of us can't help but be

distracted by wealth; that wealth makes us mad?

JN: Most assuredly I say to you, a rich man will enter into the kingdom of heaven with difficulty.

SP: They'll struggle?

JN: It's easier for a camel to go through a needle's eye than for a rich man to enter into the kingdom of God.

SP: But that's astonishing, teacher! I mean, who then can be saved?

JN: With men, this is impossible.

SP: So that's that?

JN: Impossible with men, but with God all things are possible.

SP: I see. So as I understand it, material poverty in some way helps heaven to live in us on earth.

JN: Blessed are the poor, yes.

SP: For God must fill the poor as sunlight fills the clean air?

JN: The kingdom of God is theirs.

SP: So what else hurts us, teacher? Possessions hurt us, but what else? As you know, some are very insistent with their rules about what we eat and drink.

JN: Hear and understand. That which enters into the mouth defiles no one.

SP: Is that so?

JN: It is that which proceeds *out* of the mouth, this is what defiles!

SP: I don't understand. I've always been taught –

JN: – don't you understand that whatever goes into the mouth passes into the belly and then out of the body?

SP: I suppose so.

JN: While the things which proceed out of the mouth, they come from the heart, and it is those things which defile someone. But to eat with unwashed hands? That defiles no one.

SP: The Pharisees won't like that.

JN: So then, beware of these false prophets, who appear in sheep's clothing –

SP: – or long robes.

JN: Inwardly, they are ravening wolves.

SP: But how are we to know a false prophet from a true one?

JN: By their fruits you will know them.

SP: Fair enough.

JN: Listen – salt is good.

SP: Salt is very good. Where would we be without it?

JN: But what if the salt becomes flat and tasteless? With what do you season it?

SP: There's nothing really. I mean, if salt has stopped being salty it's beyond saving.

JN: Exactly. It's fit neither for the soil nor the dung heap and is thrown out.

SP: So what are you saying? When something stops being helpful for us, whether a person, practice, or belief, we are to leave them, just as we'd throw away salt or leave a dried-up well. What was helpful once is not necessarily helpful now, and actually may cause us to stumble.

JN: Things that make people stumble are bound to happen in life.

SP: Inevitable.

JN: But woe to the Scribes and Pharisees, hypocrites!

SP: Someone said they make the unimportant, crucial and the important, unnecessary.

JN: Oh yes, they carefully tithe mint, dill, and cumin and yet completely ignore the weightier matters of the law.

SP: Which are?

JN: Justice, mercy, and trust.

sp: Beautiful attitudes.

jn: But these men are blind guides who strain out a gnat and yet swallow a camel!

sp: You have a satirical twist in you, teacher, and thank God for that. Satire keeps the powerful in check and religion is particularly open to the abuse of power; an abuse which hurts many.

jn: These people – they travel around by sea and land to make converts; and yet when they have one in their grasp, they make them twice as fit for hell as they themselves are.

sp: You don't pull your punches.

jn: They're like a dog sleeping in the manger of the cattle. They do not eat themselves but they do not let the cattle eat either.

sp: Everyone, in their way, wants power or status. I've heard it's not unknown among your followers even.

jn: The mother of the Zebedee boys came to me with her sons, kneeling and with a request on their mind. I said 'What do you want?'

sp: Status?

jn: She said, 'Command that these, my two lovely sons, may sit with you in your kingdom, one on your right hand and one on your left hand.'

sp: You do come across parents who live their lives through

their children.

JN: I said, 'You don't know what you're asking.'

SP: I do. She was asking for a couple of very big thrones.

JN: 'Are you able to drink the cup that I am about to drink,' I said, 'and be baptized with the baptism that I am baptized with?' 'We are able,' they said.

SP: The confidence of youth.

JN: So I said, 'Then you will indeed drink my cup and share my baptism, but to sit on my right hand and on my left hand is not mine to give, but for those invited there by my father.'

SP: Did your other followers hear of this?

JN: Oh yes. And when they did, they were most indignant with the two brothers.

SP: Yes, I think I can hear the reaction.

JN: But I said, 'You know how the rulers of the Gentiles lord it over their people and how their great ones exercise authority?'

SP: It's well-documented.

JN: 'But it's not going to be like that among you,' I said. 'No, for whoever desires to become great among you shall be your servant.'

SP: A new way of leading; leadership which holds rather than exploits. And no insecure showmanship or seeking of attention? You're not fond of that.

JN: Yes, be careful that your charitable giving is not for public consumption, to be seen and admired.

SP: Charitable giving as a form of self-love?

JN: So there are to be no trumpet fanfares heralding your merciful deeds, as the hypocrites do in the synagogues and streets that they may receive human approval – they have received their reward.

SP: So who's allowed to know when we do something?

JN: No one. Don't even let your left hand know what your right hand does, so that your merciful deeds may truly be secret; then your father who sees in secret will reward you openly.

SP: We find our value in our relationship to our heavenly father and not in hallucinations of self-importance fuelled by popular acclaim?

JN: Suppose you have a servant who is ploughing or looking after the sheep.

SP: Me with a servant? That's certainly hallucination.

JN: Then suppose the servant comes in from the field. Now, do you tell him to hurry, sit down and eat his meal?

SP: Would you?

JN: Of course not! Instead, you say to him, 'Get my supper

ready, then put on your apron and wait on me while I eat and drink, and after that, and only after that, you may have your meal.

SP: That's certainly how it is in the world.

JN: Well, the servant hardly deserves thanks for obeying orders, does he?

SP: I suppose not.

JN: And it's just the same with you. When you have done all you have been told to do, say only, 'We are ordinary servants; we have merely done our duty.'

SP: And for those who feel hurt by life; those who dwell on things and somehow can't get free?

JN: Be passersby.

SP: Be passersby? You mean understand that we're pilgrims, that all is impermanent, even our hurt?

JN: Be passersby.

SP: Understand that the earth is a bridge and you don't build a house on a bridge; disengage from our hurt, that whatever it is, this too will pass and we are quite well?

JN: Be passersby.

NINE

Do you have healing hands?

*I've heard various views on Jesus as a healer. A Babylonian took
me to one side to announce that Jesus of Nazareth was hanged
because in his healing and exorcism, 'he practised sorcery and had
beguiled and led Israel astray'.*

*Flavius Josephus is more favourable. In his view, Jesus is a 'wise
man' and 'a performer of astonishing deeds'. Celsus the Greek
accepts quite freely that Jesus performs miracles, but says that he
does so by the power of Satan.*

*Do miracles happen? Perhaps it depends on what you call a
miracle. Some say a miracle is when God does the will of man.
Others say it's a more extraordinary happening when man does
the will of God!*

*Such debate is for another time, however. Can a man do what
Jesus is reported to have done? Not ordinarily we might say, but
then Jesus's followers say he isn't ordinary, and that these are not
ordinary times. I can only report what I hear.*

SP: You're a healer, I understand.

JN: I give you that which eye has not seen, and ear has
not heard and hand has not touched and no human heart
conceived.

SP: Quite an opening. But this healing – it has brought you
trouble.

JN: A leper approaches me and says 'If you want to, you can

87

make me clean.'

SP: This is how it happens?

JN: I am moved with compassion, stretch out my hand, touch him and say 'I want to. Be made clean.'

SP: And what happens then?

JN: Immediately the leprosy leaves his body, and I firmly warn him, 'See that you say nothing to anyone, but go show yourself to the priest, and offer for your cleansing the thank-offering which Moses commands.'

SP: I've heard that you often tell people to stay silent about their healing. Of course, some say you cast out demons by the power of the Prince of demons.

JN: Unlikely, for surely every kingdom divided against itself collapses, just as a house divided against itself falls. So if Satan also is divided against himself, just how will his kingdom stand?

SP: Fair point.

JN: No, if by the finger of God I expel demons, then the kingdom of God has come to you.

SP: And sometimes, you link sin with sickness, teacher, inner distress with outer distress, and so heal with forgiveness. I was thinking about the 'hole in the roof' gang.

JN: A paralyzed man was brought to me by four friends, yes.

SP: I heard about this. They were trying to reach you, but couldn't find a way through the crowds, so they lowered their friend through the roof of the house where you were, ripping up the beams and the plastering.

JN: And when I saw their faith, I said to the sufferer, 'My son, your sins are forgiven.'

SP: And that's a provocative statement.

JN: Some of the Scribes were questioning me inwardly, yes.

SP: Well, they would be.

JN: 'Why does this man speak thus?' they said. 'Who can forgive sins but God alone?'

SP: That is an established principle in Jewish understanding.

JN: But I said to them, 'So tell me, which is easier: to say to the paralyzed man, "Your sins are forgiven" or to say, "Rise, pick up your stretcher and walk"'?

SP: The two are the same?

JN: But that you may know that the son of man has authority on earth to forgive sins, 'Rise, pick up your stretcher and go home.'

SP: And feel free to use the *front* door this time! A good story, teacher – though with this man, it was the faith of others, the faith of his friends that made the difference. Every healing is different.

JN: I was by the sea –

SP: – Galilee? –

JN: – when a ruler of the synagogue, Jairus, saw me, fell at my feet, and started to plead with me.

SP: What did he want?

JN: 'My little daughter is at the point of death,' he said. 'Please come and lay your hands on her that she may be made healthy and live.'

SP: So did you go? The synagogue authorities weren't always your friends.

JN: I went with him, yes, but there was a large crowd around me, pressing in on us from all sides.

SP: You do attract crowds.

JN: And then someone touched my clothes, so I turned round in the crowd and asked: 'Who touched my clothes?'

SP: How do you mean, 'Who touched my clothes?' It sounds like half of Galilee was touching your clothes.

JN: I looked to see who had done this thing and a frightened and trembling woman revealed herself.

SP: It had been her?

JN: I said 'Daughter, your faith has made you well. Go in peace, and be cured of your disease.'

SP: And what about the synagogue fellow?

JN: Jairus.

SP: Yes, Jairus. Weren't you meant to be saving his daughter?

JN: While I was still speaking, some people came from his house and said: 'Your daughter is dead. Why bother the teacher any more?'

SP: Well, you can't save everyone. Though that's the trouble with miracles: the ones that *do* happen make the ones that *don't* all the more inexplicable and painful.

JN: I immediately said to Jairus 'Don't be afraid, only believe.'

SP: Ah, James told me about this, because you allowed him, Peter, and John to follow you into the house; them and only them, he said. And of course everyone was crying, everyone distraught – you know how they wail, and on this occasion, with good reason.

JN: I said, 'Why do you make such a commotion?'

SP: I would have thought that was obvious.

JN: The child is not dead, but asleep.

SP: James says they all then turned on you, no, laughed at you.

JN: I put them all out of the house, but took the mother and father with me –

SP: — and Peter, James, and John.

JN: We went in to where the child was lying, and then taking the child by the hand, I said to her, 'talitha cum' —

SP: Meaning?

JN: Kid, get up.

SP: So what happened?

JN: Immediately the girl got up and walked, for she was twelve years old.

SP: They must have been so relieved.

JN: I ordered them quite firmly that no one should know this, and told them to give her something to eat.

TEN

The inside of the cup

I sense Jesus has mixed feelings about religion; what started as a mysterious journey home for the soul has become a rule-bound institution for the frightened. And quite how the kingdom of God relates to religion I'm not sure; maybe Jesus isn't either. On the face of it, it seems to announce a new relationship between God and humankind and fresh springs for morality. The law is not unimportant; but is no longer central.

The critics of Jesus discern, rightly enough, that his teaching is threatening. It threatens the integrity of Judaism as a system in which religion and national solidarity are inseparable. Jesus removes the old ceremonial law but doesn't replace it with a new one, which leaves a dangerous vacuum.

The real danger in Jesus is this: he has eyes for something beyond the law. It's our intention which interests Jesus, and this makes him a threat to us all.

sp: Spiritual teaching is usually something external, a call from above; but your teaching suggests the 'above' calls to us from within?

jn: A certain Pharisee asked me to dine with him.

sp: And you accepted?

jn: I went in and sat straight down at the table.

sp: You mean, without washing?

JN: Yes, and when the Pharisee saw that, he was astonished that I hadn't washed myself before dinner.

SP: And he made his astonishment plain.

JN: So I said to him 'You Pharisees clean the outside of the cup and plate, but inwardly, you remain choked with extortion and wickedness.'

SP: You are a craftsman in the art of rudeness.

JN: 'You foolish ones', I said, 'didn't the one who made the outside make the inside also?'

SP: Here is a passion of yours, teacher: our inner disposition, our wholeness of character, consistency of thought, word, and act.

JN: Of course. First clean the inside of the cup and the plate, so that the outside may become clean also.

SP: So the inner life comes first? Is this why ostentatious religion makes you choke, as it glorifies the outer life and external appearances?

JN: The whitewashing of a tomb.

SP: But people struggle with you because you're not practical. You may surpass Hillel as an ethical teacher, but your teaching is not possible in practice, and so the danger is that you leave ordinary life untouched. People will dismiss you as a poet or an idealist, and then get on with their lives as before. Maybe you're too good for us. You focus on the inner life of intention, at the expense of the daily rules offered by other moralists. You suggest attitudes we need to adopt; but refuse to give a list of things we must *do*. I mean, some people say we must fast –

JN: – if you fast you will be at fault.

SP: I beg your pardon?

JN: If you fast you will be at fault, and if you pray, you will be wrong.

SP: Yes, and that's why you unsettle people! Because just when they think they're doing something good –

JN: – and if you give to charity, you will rot your mind.

SP: Fasting, prayer, and charity – these are the bedrock of many people's faith! But perhaps I see what you're doing. You believe the great failing of moralistic religion is to end up as a series of brutalizing rules and commands that have lost sight and sense of the subtle inner textures of human existence; of the quality of the heart.

JN: I must be about my father's business.

SP: And what an unsettling business it is!

JN: From the quality of the heart, the mouth speaks.

SP: Indeed. And on the subject of unsettling people, you've lost many friends with your views on circumcision.

JN: Look, if circumcision were useful, fathers would create sons already circumcised on emerging from their mothers!

SP: You mean it's a man-made addition to the spiritual life?

JN: It's only the circumcision in spirit that is truly useful.

SP: But circumcision is a sign of distinctiveness for the Jews, precious as a mark of separation. So the question is: if not by outer signs, how are we to distinguish ourselves from others? I mean, which is the greatest commandment?

JN: Love the Lord your God with all your heart, with all your soul, and with all your mind.

SP: I thought that might be there.

JN: And love your neighbour as you love yourself.

SP: I see. And in such a climate of universal love, there is no separation from others, so no need for external distinctiveness?

JN: The whole law of Moses and the teaching of the prophets depend on these two commandments.

SP: And all Pharisees would say the same, of course, even the Shammaites. Yet you differ from them; your angle of approach is not the same. Because what I hear in your teaching is not so much a command to love God – a rather forced and cold instruction – as the call to become the child that we are.

JN: Become as a child, yes. Your father in heaven knows your needs.

SP: And be open and receptive to the kingdom within ourselves?

JN: And when you know yourself, then you will be known.

SP: A circle of understanding? Self-knowing leads to divine knowing?

JN: And then you will understand that you are the child of the living father.

SP: And if you do not know yourself?

JN: If you do not know yourself, you will live in vain and you will be vanity.

SP: That's a high price for a lack of self-knowledge. And presumably, our lack of inner awareness damages our perception of the world.

JN: Of course. You see the speck in your brother's eye, but you do not see the beam in your own eye.

SP: Our constant state.

JN: Only when you remove the beam from your own eye, will you see clearly enough to remove the speck from your brother's eye.

SP: So self-knowledge and self-correction are preferable to criticism of others; and we are to acknowledge the beam in our own eye before attempting anything. The teachers of the law and the Pharisees do not emphasize such things.

JN: The teachers of the law and the Pharisees are the authorized interpreters of Moses's law, so you must obey and follow everything they tell you to do.

SP: Really?

JN: Do not, however, imitate their actions.

SP: Why not?

JN: They do not practise what they preach.

SP: They do work hard to be ritually clean.

JN: And do you know what I say to them? Give what is in your cups and on your plates to the poor and then everything will be ritually clean for you!

SP: We're back with intentions again. It's by our intention and not our act that we are purified. Yet as you say, these people are authorized interpreters of Moses's law; they know it all.

JN: Those who know all, yet do not know themselves, are lacking everything.

SP: And that reminds me of more words from the *Dhammapada*: 'Let a person be a light to himself and learn wisdom. When he is free from delusion, he will go beyond birth and death.' As with the Buddha, a follower of yours is one with an awakened conscience, is one who –

JN: – hears these words and acts on them.

SP: Hears and acts, yes. Well, that's practical enough. And it's life and death?

JN: I saw a Samaritan carrying a lamb and entering into Judea.

s p: Not unusual.

j n: I said to my followers, 'What will the man do with the lamb?'

s p: Kill it, presumably.

j n: Yes, as long it is alive, I said, he will not eat it; he'll only eat it when he kills it and it becomes a corpse.

s p: It can hardly be otherwise.

j n: So seek for yourself a place within for rest, lest you become a corpse and be eaten.

ELEVEN

Whom are you trying to help?

You don't need me to tell you that Judea is not well. It is a state riven by faction, with a secularized priesthood subservient to Rome, while the masses live in impotent hatred of both. Religious teachers like the Pharisees, earnest in their way, only widen the gap between the pious and the despised 'people of the land'. Jesus looks with the eyes of the prophet and believes the people of God have lost their way. He sees leaders, blinded by collusion, unable to recognize the danger to the nation. So how can he help? Or rather, whom can he help?

Jesus has an inner circle of twelve, a number chosen perhaps to symbolize the twelve tribes of Israel. (He's respectful of the past even if he champions the present.) This community of twelve centres on him, but its boundaries are not firmly drawn. In the Essene community, truth is only given to enrolled members of the sect, but it's nothing like that with Jesus. He shares with anyone, and mixes freely with all, including women, tax collectors, Gentiles, and children, none of whom are traditional associates of the religious establishment.

But whom exactly is he here for? Ask ten people that question, and you get ten different answers.

SP: There's a strong sense of you being sent on a mission, teacher. But to whom have you been sent?

JN: I was sent to the lost sheep of the house of Israel.

SP: That's certainly what you told your followers in the early days.

JN: Go nowhere among the Gentiles, I said, and enter no town of the Samaritans.

SP: So at that point, nothing for the Gentiles?

JN: It is not right to take the children's bread and throw it to the dogs.

SP: What you offer is too rich for the Gentiles?

JN: Do not give dogs what is holy; and do not throw your pearls before swine.

SP: So in the early days, this was a Jews-only affair? A surprisingly narrow ambition, teacher.

JN: I said to my followers, 'Preach that the kingdom of heaven is at hand!'

SP: Though not for Gentiles or Samaritans.

JN: Take neither gold, nor silver, nor brass in your money belts. Take no bag for your journey, neither two coats, nor shoes, nor staff: for the labourer is worthy of his food.

SP: They were to travel in trust.

JN: 'Into whatever city or village you enter,' I said, 'find out who there is worthy, and stay with them until it's time to go. And as you enter into the household, greet it, and if the household is worthy, let your peace come on it, but if it isn't worthy – well then, let your peace return to you.'

SP: So no peace for the wicked? These were your instructions.

JN: 'And whoever doesn't receive you,' I told them, 'or who refuses to listen to you, then as you go out of that house or that city, shake off the dust from your feet.'

SP: A dismissive response.

JN: 'And listen well when I tell you, it will be more tolerable for the land of Sodom and Gomorrah on the judgement day than for that city.'

SP: And so with those instructions ringing in their ears, your followers went out. But so did you, teacher, and you didn't keep to your rules; or not the one about Gentiles. There was the Canaanite woman, for instance.

JN: She was crying out, 'Have mercy on me, Lord, you son of David!'

SP: A woman who wasn't Jewish, not one of the lost house of Israel, and yet there was a change of mind in you, teacher.

JN: 'My daughter is severely demonized!' she cried.

SP: And how did you answer her?

JN: I didn't answer her.

SP: But your disciples were pleading with you to send her away, because her shouting was getting on their nerves. So what did you say to her?

JN: I said I wasn't sent to anyone but the lost sheep of the house of Israel.

SP: But she was persistent, wasn't she? She didn't believe you and hung in there, saying 'Lord, help me.'

JN: I said it's just not appropriate to take the children's bread and throw it to the dogs.

SP: Which was pretty rude, but she ignored that, and said, 'Yes, Lord, but even dogs eat the crumbs which fall from their masters' table.'

JN: She did.

SP: And that worked.

JN: I said, 'Woman, great is your trust!'

SP: A trust you'd certainly tested.

JN: Imagine this. You go to a friend at midnight, and tell him, 'Friend, lend me three loaves of bread, for another friend has travelled far to see me and I have nothing to offer him.'

SP: A serious problem at that hour of the day.

JN: And suppose the owner of the house shouts down to you, 'Don't bother me, man! The door is now shut and my children and I are in bed. It's not convenient to get up and give it to you!'

SP: I'd knock and knock again –

JN: – which is just what the man did. The owner would not respond out of friendship, but because of the man's persistence, he got up and gave him as many loaves as he needed.

sp: And so it was with the woman from Tyre.

jn: Let it be done to you just as you desire, I said to her.

sp: And her daughter was healed from that moment? A Gentile healing! You see, as much as you tried to be a good Jew, you seem to have struggled with the idea. You call the Gentiles 'dogs', but then you talk with them, listen to them, eat with them, and heal them. You're a failed separatist, teacher, or to put it more positively, a man large enough to change his mind. Life is change, as they say, and to be perfect is to have changed often, because now I'm thinking of the centurion. Do you remember the centurion?

jn: When I arrived in Capernaum, a centurion approached me saying, 'Lord, my servant lies in the house paralyzed and in great pain.'

sp: Your zealot friends would have spat at a Roman, possibly worse.

jn: I said, 'I will come and heal him.'

sp: So now you're upsetting the grass roots, the nationalists.

jn: The centurion then says, 'Lord, I'm not worthy for you to come under my roof. But just say the word, and my servant will be healed. I'm a man under the authority of higher-ranked officers, but with soldiers in my command also. I tell this one, "Go," and he goes; and tell another, "Come," and he comes; and I tell my servant, "Do this," and yes, he does it!'

sp: He had confidence in a simple command from you.

JN: When I heard this, I marvelled.

SP: You liked him.

JN: I had never seen such trust, not even in Israel.

SP: That's magnanimous…for a Galilean…about a Roman.

JN: Go on your way, I said. Let it be done for you as you have believed.

SP: And it wasn't just Romans. You broke the rules with women too, some of whom travelled with you. You've got your inner circle of course. There's Simon Peter; Andrew, his brother; James; John, his brother; Philip; Bartholomew; Thomas; Matthew the tax collector; the other James, Thaddaeus, Simon the Canaanite, and Judas Iscariot, who, well – we'll return to him. But then there's also Mary Magdalene, whom you'd healed, and Joanna, the wife of Chuzas, Herod's steward; and Susanna, of course, who arranged this meeting – and they're just the ones I've spoken with. There are many other women as well; women who support you in material ways. Some Pharisees call you 'carnal', but you ignore that, because you admire these women.

JN: I was in Bethany, in the house of Simon the Pharisee.

SP: And?

JN: A woman came to me carrying an alabaster jar of very expensive ointment, and proceeded to pour it on my head as I sat at the table.

SP: And how did that go down?

JN: My followers were indignant.

SP: Surprise, surprise.

JN: 'Why this waste?' they said. 'This ointment might have been sold for a great deal of money and the proceeds given to the poor!'

SP: Such noble sentiments.

JN: I said to them, 'Why do you bother the woman when she has done a good work for me? You will always have the poor with you; but you won't always have me. In pouring this ointment on my body,' I said, 'she has prepared me for burial. And I tell you all, wherever my good news is preached in the world, what this woman has done will also be spoken of as a memorial of her.'

SP: And that was Mary Magdalene; though I can't imagine your host was very pleased.

JN: Simon is thinking, 'If this man is truly a prophet, he'll know what kind of a woman this is who touches him; he'd know that she's low-life.'

SP: Such thinking would be natural. The Essene community, whom I've had brief contact with in my travels, are perhaps the purist upholders of the Jewish religion. They remain determinedly unmarried and expressly reject three groups: women, sinners, and the weak – in fact, all the people you spend time with.

JN: Be merciful as your father in heaven is merciful.

SP: And there you agree with Rabbi Hillel: 'The Merciful inclines the scales towards mercy,' he said. But your behaviour at Simon's house was a scandal not only to the Essenes; it was a scandal to Pharisees, Sadducees, and zealots alike.

JN: Then I thank my father that he has hidden these things from the learned and wise, and revealed them to the simple.

SP: What things?

JN: I said, 'Simon –

SP: – your host –

JN: '– Simon, I have something to tell you. A certain lender had two debtors. One owed the lender five hundred denarii while the other one owed only fifty.'

SP: Five hundred is a great deal of money.

JN: But when they couldn't pay, he forgave them both. So tell me: which of them will love him most?

SP: No question: the one who he forgave the most, the one who owed five hundred.

JN: You judge correctly. And so I turned to Mary and said to Simon, 'Do you see this woman? I entered your home, and you gave me no water for my feet, yet she has wet my feet with her tears, and wiped them with the hair of her head.'

SP: Not socially acceptable and offensive to many.

JN: 'You gave me no kiss,' I said, 'but this woman, ever since the time I arrived, she has not ceased to kiss my feet.'

SP: It's getting worse.

JN: And while you didn't even think to anoint my head with oil, she has anointed my feet with ointment. So I tell you, her many sins are forgiven, for she loved much.

SP: 'She loved much'. And of course Phillip told me that this same Mary Magdalene was your – how can we say? – special companion; that you loved her more than the other disciples and would often, to use Philip's phrase, kiss her on the mouth; and that the others asked 'Why do you love her more than us?'

JN: How could it be that I did not love them as much as I love her? But know that those who are only forgiven a little, love only a little.

SP: That's true, teacher. You have to be open to forgiveness to receive forgiveness, and the frightened aren't open. They're busy justifying themselves, scared of their darkness, and too insecure to allow the cracks. They can offer fear and regulations, but as you say, they can't offer love.

JN: She loved much.

SP: So it appears. But returning to my question at the start, because it still isn't clear to me at all: to whom are you sent? Are the people of God in fact the people who don't imagine they're the people of God? You do eat with the wrong people.

JN: People who are well do not need a doctor, but only those who are sick. I have not come for the respectable people, but for those cast out to the edge.

SP: Like who?

JN: I was in the temple when the Scribes and the Pharisees brought a woman caught in the act of adultery.

SP: I heard about this. They said the Law of Moses must be satisfied which meant stoning. The man involved was not to be stoned, just the woman, for that was the law.

JN: I stooped down and wrote on the ground with my finger.

SP: Calm in a crisis.

JN: But when they continued to harass me, I looked up and said: 'He who is without sin here, let him cast the first stone at her.'

SP: And the crowd disbanded.

JN: Yes, I was now alone with the woman. She was standing where they'd left her, there in the middle. I stood up and said, 'Woman, where are your accusers? Is there no one left to condemn you?' She said, 'No one, sir.' 'Well then, neither do I condemn you – go, and sin no more.'

SP: A remarkable story and mightily embarrassing to many, I'm sure. But tell me, if you don't want the law of Moses for your people, what do you want?

JN: It is kindness I want, not animal sacrifices.

TWELVE

Do you bring peace or a sword?

There's an irenic spirit about Jesus; a man of non-violence, who in his words, 'comes not to rule but to serve'. And his stories and encounters reveal a man intensely interested in the lives of others.

But there's also a sword in his hand, sharp, prophetic, and dangerous; and with it, he cuts to the very marrow of my soul.

SP: You said 'Blessed are the peace makers.' But there's much in your teaching that doesn't bring peace.

JN: Don't think that I came to send peace on the earth. I didn't come to send peace, but a sword.

SP: The sword of exposure?

JN: I come to set a man at odds against his father, and a daughter against her mother, and a daughter-in-law against her mother-in-law. A man's enemies will be those of his own household.

SP: Yes, that isn't peace.

JN: He who loves father or mother more than me is not worthy of me; and he who loves son or daughter more than me isn't worthy of me.

SP: We've spoken already about families. I understand they can have a vested interest in holding you back from discovery and from new ways of looking at things. But do you also describe here our inner household? We're put at odds with our inner selves, that we might be loosened from, and take leave of, our old selves.

JN: Seek and you will discover; discover and you shall be disturbed.

SP: Yes, and this disturbance within feels like a sword.

JN: You have heard that it was said, 'You shall not murder'.

SP: Of course.

JN: But I tell you again, that everyone who is angry with his brother without a cause shall be in danger of the judgement, and whoever says, 'You fool!' shall be in danger of the fires of hell.

SP: When you speak like this, you destroy us all.

JN: And you have heard it said, 'You shall not commit adultery.'

SP: The seventh commandment.

JN: But I tell you that everyone who gazes lustfully at a woman has already committed adultery with her in his heart.

SP: Then we are all adulterers.

JN: And again you have heard that people were told in the past, 'Do not break your promise, but do what you have vowed to the Lord to do.'

SP: Certainly!

JN: But I tell you, do not use any vow when you make a promise.

SP: Really? My friend swears on his mother's life – but somehow remains unreliable.

JN: Do not swear at all. Do not swear by heaven, for it is the throne of God; nor by the earth, for it is the footstool of his feet; nor by Jerusalem, for it is the city of the great King. Do not even swear by your head, for you cannot make one hair on it white or black.

SP: So what are we to do?

JN: Let your 'yes' be 'yes' and your 'no' be 'no.' Anything more is of the evil one.

SP: A simple 'yes' and a simple 'no'.

JN: And you've heard it said, 'An eye for an eye and a tooth for a tooth.'

SP: That's exactly what a fish-seller told me just last night, after he'd taken revenge on his neighbour.

JN: But I tell you, don't resist him who is evil.

SP: Really?

JN: And if someone slaps your right cheek, offer him the other as well.

SP: The fish-seller was attacked! He has knife wounds on his face. He had to fight back, as all sensible people understand.

I'm sorry, but I think I'm with the Pharisee who said this 'turning the other cheek' thing is a diseased upheaval of moral law.

JN: And if anyone takes you to court to get your shirt, then let him have your cloak also.

SP: I don't see that happening.

JN: And whoever compels you to go one mile, go with him two. Give to him who asks you, and don't turn away any who desire to borrow from you.

SP: You will make simpletons of us! Laughing stock!

JN: And finally, do for others what you want them to do for you.

SP: We're on more solid ground here. You echo Hillel's words, in a way. 'That which is hateful to you,' he says, 'do not do to your fellow. That is the whole of the Torah; the rest is explanation, go and learn.' But you phrase the command more positively.

JN: Do for others what you want them to do for you: this is the meaning of the Law of Moses and the teaching of the prophets. Bless those who curse you, do good to those who hate you, and pray for those who mistreat you and persecute you.

SP: But why?

JN: That you may be children of your father in heaven.

SP: You mean until then we are not? You say that such unconditional love – my rabbi friends would call it impractical love, impossible in the real world – such love is the defining characteristic of God's children?

JN: Of course. Be perfect like your heavenly father is perfect.

SP: So we're not to keep accounts against anyone, because our heavenly father keeps no accounts.

JN: Doesn't he make his sun rise on the evil and the good?

SP: He does.

JN: And sends rain on the just and the unjust.

SP: True.

JN: And really, if you love only those who love you, what is in that? Don't even the tax collectors do the same?

SP: Probably, yes.

JN: And if you only greet your friends, what more do you do than others do? Don't even the tax collectors do the same?

SP: So nothing too challenging then: you just want us to be perfect, and I trust you can hear the sarcasm in my voice.

JN: Yes, be perfect as your father in heaven is perfect.

SP: You expose us, dismantle us, and bid us be perfect? You bring something, teacher, but it isn't peace.

JN: Salt is good, but if the salt has lost its saltiness, with what will you season it? Have salt in yourselves and be as one with each other.

THIRTEEN

Are you lonely?

I was told that sometimes when they were walking together, Jesus would be found ahead of his followers. I found this gap between them quite revealing.

SP: No teacher can share their consciousness, which must make yours a lonely path. Do you feel lonely?

JN: Jerusalem, Jerusalem!

SP: You were never at home here.

JN: In Jerusalem they kill the prophets and stone the messengers God sends; yet how often I longed to put my arms around these people.

SP: This is a troubled city.

JN: Like a hen gathers her chicks beneath her wings, so would I have gathered her children together. But –

SP: – but what?

JN: They would not let me.

SP: No. But then you cannot share a way of being, teacher. You can share words, but you can't share your understanding of those words; that's an individual journey, requiring some bravery. So for much of the time, your message hits the thick barriers of habitual reaction and conventional thought – as in your story of the four soils. And the rejection started in

Nazareth of course, your hometown. We've touched on this.

JN: Ah yes. 'Isn't he the carpenter?' they'd say – 'the son of Mary and the brother of James, Joseph, Judas, and Simon? And aren't his sisters living here?'

SP: Which of course they were.

JN: A prophet is never welcomed in his hometown or by his family and relatives.

SP: They all think they know you.

JN: And no one is a doctor in their own home.

SP: They'd labelled you, put you in a box, and didn't want you out of it. How do you cope with that?

JN: There's a place where I am not persecuted, and that place they will never find.

SP: So no one knows where Jesus goes, when Jesus goes away? You have an inner place they can't reach. But even so, you left Nazareth never to have a home again.

JN: Foxes have their holes and birds have their nests, but the son of man has nowhere to lay his head.

SP: It was a precarious path you and your followers took. At the height of your popularity, of course, there were great hopes that you would lead a national revolt.

JN: My kingdom is not of this world.

SP: No. And when you refused to be this leader, there were defections and you became more reliant on your inner circle. You took them out of Galilee, away from Herod's threatening domain and the restrictive atmosphere of synagogues. And perhaps a degree of anonymity was helpful for a while, in the Gentile territory of Tyre. Though ironically, it was your friends and not your enemies who would highlight your isolation. One of your closest friends, Peter –

JN: Peter said 'Even if everyone else denies you, I will never deny you!'

SP: This was towards the end, when the authorities were closing in.

JN: I said, 'I tell you that tonight, Peter, before the rooster crows, you will deny me three times.'

SP: And did he believe you?

JN: No. He said, 'Even if I must die with you, I will not deny you!' And all the others said the same.

SP: That's Peter for you, and he's still a bit of a blusterer. But you were arrested soon after and taken away, after which your followers scattered. What were your worst moments?

JN: Before the arrest, we had come together to a place called Gethsemane.

SP: The garden?

JN: I said, 'Stay here, while I go pray.' I took Peter, James, and John –

SP: – the inner circle –

JN: – but felt overwhelmed by sorrow and forebodings. I said this to them. I said, 'My soul is exceedingly sad, even to death. Stay here, my friends, and watch with me.'

SP: And then?

JN: I walked forward a little, fell on my face and prayed, 'My father, if it is possible, let this cup pass away from me; nevertheless, not what I desire, but what you desire.'

SP: You sensed a dark future closing in on you? At least you had company.

JN: My followers were sleeping.

SP: Oh.

JN: I said to Peter, 'Could you not watch with me for just one hour? Watch and pray that you don't enter into temptation. The spirit indeed is willing, but the flesh is weak.'

SP: And then?

JN: A second time I went away to pray, 'My father, if this cup cannot be taken from me unless I drink it, your will be done.'

SP: This was not mere loneliness, but a collapsing future, like a fox at the end of its run. The heart of darkness was at hand.

JN: I returned to my friends, but they were sleeping again, heavy-eyed. So I left them again and prayed a third time, saying the same words.

SP: And your snoring followers? I mean, how did you feel?

JN: How long shall I be with you? How long must I endure you? Don't you understand?

SP: These were desperate times.

JN: So I said, 'Sleep on now and take your rest! Behold, the hour is at hand, and the son of man is betrayed into the hands of sinners.'

SP: I know the Gethsemane garden. I'll never walk it again without thinking of that night, when it became for you the garden of loneliness, the garden of sadness.

JN: Many are standing by the door, but only those who are alone and solitary can enter the bridal chamber.

SP: I'm sorry?

JN: Many are standing by the door, but only those who are alone and solitary can enter the bridal chamber.

SP: You're saying that many speak of love and dream of love, but few go through the door; only those who have found the other, their loved one, in solitude.

JN: Close the door.

SP: Indeed. But surely this solitary strength was tested on the cross? The crowds of well-wishers had melted away, even your followers had scattered. Only four stood with you, including your mother, John, and Mary Magdalene. Here was the loneliest and most meaningless of endings.

JN: Eli, Eli, lama sabachthani?

SP: Are you saying what I think you're saying?

JN: My God, my God, why have you forsaken me!

FOURTEEN

How will it end?

*Apocalyptic imagery about the end of the world is not something
particular to Jesus; he shares it with many others. What is
distinctive with Jesus is the way he drags the End Times into the
present. The kingdom of God is here, now. A decision is urgent
and delay is dangerous. A consummation awaits, but in the
meantime, no circumstance of daily life, no encounter, feeling, or
task, is too trivial to be a window on eternity.*

SP: So tell me, teacher, what will be our end?

JN: What do you know of the beginning, so that you now
seek the end?

SP: I don't know. Is the beginning important?

JN: Where the beginning is, there will the end be also.

SP: You mean we return to where we started?

SP: Blessed are those who abide in the beginning, for they will
know the end and not taste death. Become as children.

SP: You make me think of the circle, teacher, in which each
beginning is an ending. Every point in the circle is both a
beginning and an end, as is every moment; a taking up and
a letting go. If we attend to the present in this way, the end
looks after itself?

JN: The heavens and earth will roll up before you.

S P: Is that so? I understand, of course, that we must use picture language.

J N: The living who come from the Living will experience neither fear nor death, for as it is said: the world cannot contain those with self-knowledge.

S P: And those without this knowledge?

J N: He who has in his hand, to him shall be given; and he who has not, from him shall be taken even the little that he has.

S P: If we offer nothing, God has nothing to work with?

J N: And not everyone who says to me, 'Lord, Lord,' will enter into the kingdom of heaven; but only those who do the will of my father. For the son of man will come in the glory of his father with his angels; and then he will render to everyone according to their deeds.

S P: By our fruits we will be known?

J N: I tell you that every idle word that people speak, they will give account of it in the Day of Judgement. For by your words you will be justified and by your words you will be condemned.

S P: Our words flow from our heart; so our words describe our heart more clearly than anything?

J N: Many will tell me in that day, 'Lord, Lord, didn't we prophesy in your name, in your name cast out demons, and in your name do many mighty works?' Then I will tell them, 'I never knew you. Depart from me, you wicked people!'

SP: Because ultimately, truth cannot collude with untruth, and this is the frightening light of the new kingdom.

JN: Everyone is purified by fire as a sacrifice is purified by salt.

SP: And in the flames, untruth must dissolve into truth, be received by truth – or forever wander alone in terrible isolation?

JN: When the son of man comes in his glory, the nations will be assembled before him, and he will separate them one from another, as a shepherd separates the sheep from the goats.

SP: The division bell tolls.

JN: He will set the sheep on his right hand, but the goats on the left. Then the King will tell those on his right hand, 'Come, blessed of my father, inherit the kingdom prepared for you from the foundation of the world; for I was hungry, and you gave me food to eat; I was thirsty, and you gave me drink; I was a stranger, and you took me in; naked, and you clothed me; I was sick, and you visited me; I was in prison, and you came to me.'

SP: But how could they have done all these things for God?

JN: I tell you, inasmuch as they did it to the least of my children, they did it to me.

SP: God is the one we don't pay much attention to?

JN: Then he will say also to those on the left hand, 'Depart

from me, you cursed, into the eternal fire which is prepared for
the devil and his angels; for I was hungry, and you didn't give
me food to eat; I was thirsty and you gave me no drink; I was
a stranger and you didn't take me in; naked and you didn't
clothe me; sick and in prison, and you didn't visit me.'

SP: And they'll say 'When was this so?'

JN: I tell you, inasmuch as you refused it to the least of my
children, you refused it to me.

SP: And that will be that? Meanness of spirit proves an
expensive luxury.

JN: Yes, the kingdom of heaven is like a dragnet which
fishermen throw into the sea. They catch fish of every kind,
and when the net is full, they pull it up onto the beach. They
then sit down, and throw the good fish into buckets, but
throw the bad away. So will it be in the end of the world.

SP: And will the end of the old world be the beginning of a
new one, a different one?

JN: The old man will not hesitate to ask a little child of seven
days about the place of life and he shall live.

SP: An upside-down kingdom?

JN: Indeed, and one in which many of the first will make
themselves last and they shall become one.

SP: So we are to be ready?

JN: Be like men watching for the return of their master from

125

the marriage feast; so that when he returns, they are ready to open the door to him.

SP: Not snoring on the stairs.

JN: How happy are those servants whom the master finds awake and ready on his return. I tell you, he will take off his coat, sit them down, and serve them himself!

SP: That is some homecoming.

JN: How happy they are if they are found ready, whether he comes at midnight or even later! So as I say, be ready, for the son of man is coming in an hour that you don't expect him.

SP: We carry on waiting; we scan the horizon.

JN: Yet what you wait for has already come.

SP: It's already here?

JN: What you wait for has already come, but you do not see it.

SP: Help me to see.

JN: My followers asked me this: when will that day be when you appear to us?

SP: That's what we all want to know.

JN: I said 'On the day when you are naked as newborn infants who trample their clothing.'

SP: That is when you'll appear to them? When they are naked

like newborn infants? Presumably, clothes here symbolize all that obscures or veils our essential selves. So we return to the child and trample on these things; we return to our nakedness and discover that this – and this only – is the condition for seeing you. So the End Times could be now?

JN: On the day when you are naked as newborn infants.

SP: We are back where we started, teacher. Back in the future that is now. Back with the circle, where each point, each moment, is both beginning and end – what some call the eternal now.

FIFTEEN

Into the heart of darkness

Talking with a living man about how he died is an unusual experience. But this, apparently, is what I do now. You must make your own mind up about these things. I just report what is in front of me.

The story is this: Jesus was killed on Skull Hill, just outside the city, on charges of blasphemy. Who knows the real reasons for his execution? These are not sane times. But there seems little doubt that it was the temple incident that finally did for him.

I have heard many accounts of his final days. The arrest, trial, death, and events following – these are all his friends want to talk about at the moment. But what does Jesus have to say?

SP: Let's just establish one or two things, teacher, about your last days. You timed your arrival in Jerusalem to coincide with the season of Passover, when the Romans here are particularly nervous and lay on extra garrisons. This is a time when huge numbers of Jewish pilgrims from around the world are present in the city. So anything you did at this time would receive the widest publicity for yourself.

JN: My teaching is not mine, but is from he who sent me.

SP: Indeed, but there was a plan, because a donkey was left tethered in Bethany.

JN: I sent two of my disciples, saying 'Go into the village opposite, where you will find a donkey, on which no one has ever yet sat. Untie it and bring it here and if anyone should ask why you are doing this, simply say that the master has need of it.'

SP: And so, like many others, you rode into Jerusalem on a donkey. It's pretty common at festival time, of course. Passover donkey-drivers are a breed apart and do a flourishing trade transporting pilgrims. The rich like to show off and be taken right up as far as the temple, to demonstrate their higher social status. And you also made for the temple, but with a slightly different agenda. So tell me again what happened.

JN: I entered the temple and began to drive out the buyers and the sellers there.

SP: As you've said, you overturned tables and kicked over stools. I mean, I know they put the prices up at Passover –

JN: – I said 'It is written that my house shall be a house of prayer; but you have made it into a den of robbers.'

SP: You even barred people from carrying anything through the courtyards, which must have required great courage and an intimidating presence. You were a man possessed, a terrible fury. Some said they'd never seen such clean anger.

JN: If I testify on my own behalf, what proof is there? But there is another who speaks up for me and I know what he says is true.

SP: You claim to be one with your heavenly father, I know. But your charge on this occasion was that both religion and commerce – sometimes hard to separate – were exploiting the sanctity of the temple and the gullibility of the pilgrims to make it the bastion of a powerful and exclusive faction.

JN: My teaching is not mine, you understand, but belongs to him who sent me. He who speaks on his own authority seeks his own glory.

SP: Wherever your authority comes from, you now spoke daringly, using words which even some of your followers are too embarrassed to pass on. Only John openly admits your claim.

JN: 'Destroy this temple,' I said, 'and in three days I will raise it again.'

SP: An insanely provocative thing to say.

JN: What I say is what the father has told me to say.

SP: Yet despite this temple rage and the restless crowds, you made no attempt to stir them up against the authorities? You left the temple that evening and returned to your lodgings. It was the worship of God, not the independence of the Jewish state, you were concerned with.

JN: My kingdom is not of this world.

SP: And then this meal I've heard so much about. They call it 'the last supper', and it left quite an impression. How did that come about?

JN: I sent Peter and John to go and prepare the Passover meal. They asked me where I wanted them to get it ready.

SP: And again, you'd made plans.

JN: I said, 'Go into the city where a man carrying a jar will meet you. Follow him into the house that he enters, and say to the owner of the house: "The teacher says, 'Where is the room where my followers and I will eat the Passover meal?'" He'll show you a large, furnished room upstairs, where you are to make preparation.'

SP: You made much of the bread and the wine apparently?

JN: When the hour had come, I took my place at the table with my followers –

SP: – like many others in Jerusalem on Passover night, when Israel remembers the angel of death passing over their homes in Egypt.

JN: I took the cup, gave thanks to God and said, 'Take this and share it among yourselves, for I tell you that from now on, I will not drink from the fruit of the vine until the kingdom of God comes.'

SP: You sensed this was a meal of farewell, that you were not far now from the end?

JN: I then took the bread, gave thanks and broke it and passed it around, saying, 'This is my body which is given for you. Do this in memory of me.'

SP: A keepsake?

JN: Likewise, after supper, I took the cup and said, 'This cup is the new covenant, sealed with my blood, which is poured out for you. But look!'

SP: Look?

JN: 'The hand of him who betrays me rests on this very table.'

SP: So Judas was there? Were the others aware of his intentions?

JN: No, they all began to debate among themselves, which of them it was who could possibly do such a thing?

SP: And your arrest later on the Mount of Olives, which I'm told was a familiar meeting point for you all?

JN: Yes, we left the city and went as we usually did to the Mount of Olives.

SP: We've talked about what happened there in the Gethsemane garden; how not even Peter, James and John could stay awake in your final hours together.

JN: 'Father, if you will, take this cup of suffering away from me.'

SP: And I'm thinking, teacher, of the much-loved story in Genesis when Abraham is about to kill his son Isaac. Did you ever think of that story? God has told Abraham to sacrifice his son and so, in obedience, he raises the knife in the air, ready to bring it down for the kill. But at the last moment, God intervenes to save Isaac's life. He tells Abraham to stop, and provides a ram for sacrifice instead, and allows Isaac to go free. But for you, teacher, there was no last-minute reprieve; no one to intervene on your behalf and no convenient ram.

JN: While I was still speaking to my followers, a crowd approached us led by Judas. He came up to me and kissed me. I said, 'Do you betray me with a kiss, Judas?'

SP: That was how you were identified? Betrayed with a kiss?

JN: I said to them, 'You come armed with swords and clubs as if I were some bandit! Yet I was with you in the temple daily, and you never laid a finger on me. But this is your hour and the authority of darkness.'

SP: And sometimes the darkness does have authority.

JN: They seized me and led me away to the house of the high priest.

SP: They convened the court there, and got you on the charge of blasphemy.

JN: A witness came forward and said, 'This fellow said, "I am able to destroy the temple of God and build it again in three days."'

SP: Music to their ears.

JN: The high priest stood up and said, 'Have you no answer? What is this they testify against you?'

SP: And your response?

JN: I remained silent.

SP: Silent?

JN: I remained silent. And then the high priest is saying to me, 'I put you under oath before the living God: tell us if you are the messiah, the Son of God?' 'You have said so,' I say. 'But I tell you, from now on you will see the son of man seated at the right hand of power and coming on the clouds of heaven.'

SP: I'm sure that went down well.

JN: The high priest is tearing at his clothes and saying 'He has blasphemed! Why do we still need witnesses? You yourselves have heard his blasphemy! What is your verdict?'

SP: The blasphemy charge suggests deep revulsion against you, teacher – a deep hate conditioned and fuelled by background, training, and habit. Fear and loathing in religious clothing.

JN: 'He deserves death' they answered.

SP: And blasphemy was a capital offence in Jewish law. But of course they had a problem: the Romans weren't at all interested in blasphemy against a small provincial god. So Caiaphas, the High Priest, also found a charge that would work for the Roman court.

JN: Are you the messiah?

SP: That was it. The title 'Messiah' could readily be translated into 'king of the Jews', which of course no Roman governor could ignore, particularly at the Passover festival. Messianic claims were treason, which is why Pilate asked you the same question.

JN: They took me to Pilate and made their accusations: 'We caught this man encouraging people to riot and to refuse the payment of taxes to Caesar, saying that he is the messiah, our king!'

SP: Pilate listens.

JN: 'And *are* you the king of the Jews?' he asks. 'Those are your words,' I reply.

SP: A subtle answer, teacher. But Jerusalem at Passover, defined by hate and fear – this was not a place that could handle subtlety.

JN: Whoever sees into the world discovers the body. But the world is unworthy of whoever discovers the body.

SP: You perhaps saw into the world too well. You made the comfortable feel uncomfortable and paid the price, joining the others crucified at the place they called the 'Skull'. A couple of criminals either side of you, and the usual mockery from the crowd.

JN: 'Father, forgive these people; they don't know what they're doing!'

SP: Yes, that's what I heard you said. Remarkable, because on one level they knew exactly what they were doing.

JN: They didn't know what they were doing.

SP: On another level, perhaps you're right. You saw through to their innocence; saw through the layers of hate and fear to their original charm. And is this experience of innocence the hundredth sheep you leave the other ninety-nine to find?

JN: The pearl of great price.

SP: To know yourself innocent and others innocent, even the criminal alongside you who joined in the taunting.

135

JN: But not the other one.

SP: I'm amazed you heard him.

JN: 'Remember me when you come in your power!' he said.

SP: Is it never too late to turn round?

JN: 'Today you will be with me in paradise,' I said.

SP: Words of comfort for him, teacher, but what comfort for you? You felt yourself forsaken, forsaken by your God. While all the time, your mother looked on, and with John standing alongside her, you called out.

JN: 'This man is now your son!' I said, 'And she is now your mother!'

SP: So as you died, you gave birth to a new family, giving your mother Mary another son and John a mother? I have heard she's now living in John's house. But for you, then, it was all over; your enemies had got their way.

JN: A landowner once planted a vineyard.

SP: Another story?

JN: He built a wall around it and dug a pit to crush the grapes in. He built also a lookout tower and then rented out the vineyard and left the country. Now, when it was harvest time, the owner of the vineyard sent some of his servants –

SP: – to get his share of the grapes, of course.

J N : But those renting the property grabbed the servants beating one, killing one, and stoning another to death. So the owner sends other servants, and they do exactly the same thing again.

S P : This is a bloody story.

J N : So finally, the owner sends his own son to the renters, reckoning that they would at least respect him. But when they saw the son –

S P : – they thought if we kill him, the vineyard is ours.

J N : So yes, they grabbed him, hauled him out of the vineyard, and killed him.

S P : Terrible.

J N : Now tell me –

S P : Yes?

J N : When the owner arrives, what do you imagine he will do to those renters?

S P : I see where the story's going, teacher. The revolting renters get their just deserts. Yet here's the rub – when you hung on the cross, you forgave them! 'Forgive them, father – they don't know what they're doing!' Those were your words about the people who put you there; people who seem uncannily similar to the renters. It seems you live a bigger truth than some of your stories tell.

SIXTEEN

Is there life after death?

I am sitting with a dead man who appears to be alive. He's keeping in the shadows, I grant you, but he isn't a corpse, and I've spoken to many of his shamed followers who make the same claim. How do they come to be so convinced? The first answer they give is the empty tomb. No one has found the body of the crucified Jesus. The second answer is that he's been seen alive in some manner by a number of followers.

It's hard to piece events together from their various versions, but it does seem Mary Magdalene was the first to find the tomb empty. She then told the others, who didn't believe her. Peter and another disciple, probably John, ran to the tomb for verification and found it just as Mary had told them, and they 'saw and believed'. And then of course the appearances started. They all claim, without exception, to have seen Jesus.

For his followers, it's been energizing; the recovery of a personal relationship which had seemed broken and lost forever. Some will say this is mere wish-fulfillment, and perhaps it is; but there's no doubt they are new men and women, confident and courageous, if also baffled.

SP: I have no desire to cause offence, teacher, but everyone's going to ask: 'Did you really die?' and 'Is this a real resurrection?' Lucian just thinks your followers gullible. He calls them 'misguided creatures who start with the general conviction that they are immortal for all time.' He has a point. And the Sadducees deny life beyond death as well.

JN: They came to me once.

SP: The Sadducees?

JN: They said, 'Teacher' –

SP: – I love the mock respect –

JN: – Moses said, 'If a married man dies leaving no children, his brother shall marry his widow, and have children on behalf of his brother.'

SP: That's the law, yes.

JN: Now, they said, there were once seven brothers. The first marries and dies, and having no children leaves his wife to his brother. But the second brother also dies, as does the third, and all the others down to the seventh and after them all, the woman dies. So, in the resurrection, whose wife will she be of the seven? For she had been married to them all!

SP: A tricky one. You do hear women saying how eager they are to be with their husband again, but in this case, it wasn't straightforward. They're trying to make you look foolish of course. So what was your answer?

JN: I said they were utterly mistaken, knowing neither the Scriptures nor the power of God. For in the resurrection they will neither marry nor be given in marriage, but are like God's angels in heaven.

SP: So marriage is for this life, and in the next life things are quite different.

JN: And concerning the resurrection of the dead, I said, haven't you understood what God said to you? 'I am the God of Abraham and the God of Isaac and the God of Jacob?'

sp: All great figures from the past.

jn: And God is not the God of the dead, but of the living!

sp: You mean they live on?

jn: As I say, God is not the God of the dead.

sp: It's strange, teacher. Sitting here with you now, it's as though I see a crack in the sky, picture language of course, through which some mysterious beyond beckons. It's a crack spilling light though perhaps more frightening than reassuring.

jn: Seek first the kingdom of God and all else will be given you.

sp: Mary Magdalene was frightened when you appeared to her. She told me. She'd come to your grave on the Sunday morning, just as the sun was rising, to anoint the dead body.

jn: I said 'Mary'.

sp: And she said she thought you were the gardener at first.

jn: I said 'Mary,' and she turned to me and said 'Teacher!'

sp: She recognized the voice, if not the figure.

jn: I said 'Don't hold onto me.'

sp: She must have reached out for you in shock.

J N: I said, 'Don't hold onto me. I have not yet gone to the father. But tell my followers that I am going to the one who is my father and my God.'

S P: Some will be surprised you appeared first to a woman, surprised that you relied on a woman's testimony. After all, a woman's word is not even recognized in a court of law. But then maybe you aren't concerned. When did small-mindedness ever hold you back? I mean, it crucified you but it didn't change your message.

J N: On judgement day, the Queen of the South will stand up and accuse this generation.

S P: The Queen of Sheba?

J N: For she came from the ends of the earth to hear the wisdom of Solomon –

S P: – famously wise and wealthy –

J N: – and know this: something greater than Solomon is here.

S P: Something greater than Solomon? I'm not sure your followers believed that after your death, holed up in some sweaty attic, terrified they were next for crucifixion. You visited them too, I'm told.

J N: 'Why are you troubled?' I said.

S P: You have a wicked sense of humour.

J N: 'Why do you doubt?' I said. 'See my hands and my feet, that it's truly me. Touch me and see, for ghosts don't have such flesh and bones as I have.'

SP: They must have been in shock, or perhaps just insanely happy?

JN: 'Do you have anything here to eat?' I asked.

SP: And apparently, despite their delirium, they found some baked fish –

JN: – which I took and ate in their presence, yes.

SP: And they believe it, teacher; they truly believe that you've risen from the dead. The world knows it's impossible, but they believe it, not from vague mystical experiences – God spare us from those – but from actual recognition. These are men discredited by their desertion of you, yet now both embarrassed and delighted that they have the chance to know you again.

JN: A strong city built upon a high mountain cannot be destroyed, cannot be hidden.

SP: Are you saying that death could not hold you; that there is dying but no death? The seed dies in the disgrace of the dark earth, yet rises in the glory of the morning sun? Your stories from nature are full of things that die and rise.

JN: So the kingdom of heaven is like a grain of mustard, the tiniest of all seeds. When it falls upon well-ploughed land, it becomes a great tree, where birds of the sky take shelter.

SP: And here is mystery beyond words.

JN: There are many who stand round the well, but no one goes down into it.

SP: But you did, teacher; you lowered yourself down into the darkness and found water.

SEVENTEEN

Who are you?

In many ways, Jesus fails to stand out. He is every inch a Jew in upbringing, outlook, and teaching; just another Rabbi in a land full of rabbis. And as for his end, it's sadly common also: many Jewish radicals have been crucified in recent years. He's just one more.

Despite this, however, I sense an increasing momentum to label him as someone apart. Jesus is becoming one of those people everyone has an opinion about. The Roman Jew Josephus calls him a 'wise man,' while the Syrian stoic Mara bar Serapion talks of Jesus as 'the crucified sage.' He has no time for talk of resurrections, but he did say to me that Jesus, along with Socrates and Pythagoras, was one of three wise men killed before their time.

As I say, everyone is coming to an opinion about Jesus, not least his followers. But what is the opinion of Jesus about himself?

SP: John the Baptist said that he must decrease and you must increase. So whom do you compare yourself with?

JN: I said to my disciples, 'What am I like to you? To what would you compare me?'

SP: And what did they say?

JN: Simon Peter said 'You are like a good angel.'

SP: How heavenly.

JN: Matthew said, 'You are like a wise philosopher.'

SP: Earthier, but still good.

JN: And Thomas said, 'Master, my mouth could never utter what you are like.'

SP: Well, I prefer that one. I always feel that labelling people makes fools of us all in the end.

JN: I said to Thomas, 'I am your master no longer, because you have drunk from, and become intoxicated by, the same sparkling source from which I spring.'

SP: So perhaps it's best to say nothing about you, teacher – though Herod thinks you're John the Baptizer come back to life. But stepping back for a moment, it would help if I could just gather my thoughts. I'm trying to understand you – I wouldn't be here if I wasn't – but I'm not sure how well I'm doing. Because what have we got so far? We've got a man who called his followers to cut loose from home, family, and livelihood, and commit themselves to an insecure and precarious existence; and all for a cause they barely understood.

JN: He who is near me is near the fire.

SP: They found in you a natural leader, as did others. In Galilee, the crowd asked you to lead them in nationalist revolt; they were content to follow you in a dangerous adventure, which means they trusted you. And then here in Jerusalem, in the temple, the bastion of Israel's nationhood and religion, you drove out the traders by sheer moral force – and a small whip. That's both courage and authority.

JN: My teaching is not mine.

SP: You speak as one privy to God's mind, teacher. Perhaps you are God? Perhaps you are a messiah of some sort? Some are starting to say this, but you seem hesitant to accept that title, commanding secrecy all the time.

JN: Who do people say I am?

SP: Well, as I say, some, like Herod, say John the Baptist, others Elijah, and others still, that you're one of the prophets.

JN: Peter said, 'You are the messiah.'

SP: And your response?

JN: I told him not to tell anyone.

SP: Maybe people need messiahs more than the kingdom of God needs them.

JN: The kingdom of God is like this: a farmer scatters seed in his field. He then goes to sleep, pursues his business the next day, and all the while, the seed sprouts and grows, even though he doesn't know how. And how is this so?

SP: I suppose the soil does its work.

JN: Indeed. It is the soil that works, bringing first the young stalk, then the ear, then the full grain in the ear. And when the corn is ready, then the farmer takes his sickle because it's harvest time.

SP: So the kingdom is a slow arrival, a gentle arrival even, like seed growing in the ground, without the need for loud messiahs.

JN: If I glorify myself, it is nothing.

SP: No, but you can't hide the impact and authority of your mission.

JN: It is my father who glorifies me.

SP: So you say. But whether it's even worth being the messiah of such a small and disregarded nation as Palestine is open to question. And the title does carry unhelpful baggage. It's closely associated with a military and political role, echoes of King David – and that isn't your vision at all.

JN: No, the kingdom of God is within.

SP: Exactly, and messianic language merely distracts people from that. They start hallucinating about political freedom or religious supremacy and forget about the light and darkness within themselves, the wheat and the tares of their own souls.

JN: Notice what is in your sight and what is hidden from you will be revealed.

SP: You ask us to notice, to pay attention, to be present to that which we are. So now I'm thinking that perhaps my question is the wrong question. I shouldn't be asking 'Do you claim to be the messiah?' because I can't think of a helpful answer you can give. Anyway, as God's children, we're all messiahs, surely? Instead, I should ask, 'What *kind* of a messiah do you intend to be?' That's much more interesting. What is the shape of your messiahship?

Conversations with... Jesus of Nazareth

JN: If anyone wants to be great, he must be the servant of the rest.

SP: So you say, but that's a very fresh take on the matter. Most religious people seek preferment of some sort, so in my experience, it's quite unlike the holy to end up full of holes. Yet this is what's happened to you, quite literally.

JN: So if someone wants to be first, they must be the servant of all. For the son of man did not come to be served; he came to serve.

SP: Young Mark sees this understanding in you. He links you with the figure of the 'suffering servant' in the prophet Isaiah. You'll know the prophet's words better than I.

JN: 'We despised and rejected him; he endured suffering and pain.'

SP: Yes, that's it, there in Isaiah chapter 53.

JN: 'No one would even look at him – we ignored him as if he were nothing. Yet he endured the suffering that should have been ours, the pain that we should have carried. All the while we thought his suffering was a punishment sent by God. Yet because of *our* failings he was wounded, beaten because of the evil *we* did. We are healed by the punishment he suffered; made whole by the blows he received.'

SP: It's a fair description of your last days, teacher. You're certainly not a messiah anyone was expecting.

JN: A grain of wheat remains a solitary grain unless it falls into the ground and dies.

SP: This may be true, yet most of us do the exact opposite; most of us organize our lives in such a way that we *don't* have to die. We are survivors, teacher, with our psyche, so well-described by the Greeks, erecting defences every day, to maintain our sense of control. But not you – once arrested, you laid aside all defences and relinquished all control.

JN: So! The stone the builders rejected becomes the cornerstone.

SP: You do have a capacity to turn things on their head.

JN: They search the face of heaven and earth yet do not recognize the one who is in their presence.

SP: You're too well-disguised.

JN: And more than that –

SP: – more than that? –

JN: – they do not know how to live the present moment.

SP: And our inability to live the present moment – that's the greater tragedy for us?

JN: Listen. When you see a cloud coming up in the west, at once you say it is going to rain – and it does.

SP: We're all weather forecasters at heart.

JN: And when you feel the south wind blowing, you say that it's going to get hot – and it does.

SP: Very hot.

JN: Hypocrite!

SP: Me?

JN: Hypocrite!

SP: I'm on your side!

JN: You can consider the earth and sky and foretell the weather.

SP: Well, usually; I'm not always right.

JN: Then why don't you know the meaning of the present time?

SP: Why? Well, it's hard to be present. Like most people, I prefer to pick over the past or imagine the future. Perhaps I haven't noticed this until now, noticed how rarely I'm present.

JN: Then as I say, notice what is in your sight and what is hidden from you shall be revealed.

EIGHTEEN

And what now?

SP: I've seen what happens to inspirational people like you, teacher. Your message is *developed* somewhat. Accretions and elaborations occur, for the best of religious reasons; and I'm concerned this is made easier by the fact you've written nothing down.

JN: The things that are considered of great value in the world are worth nothing in God's sight.

SP: And I'm concerned also that even now your followers talk about what you did, instead of trying to understand the energies within you which created these actions. This worries me. More than what you did, we need to know who you are, teacher. We do not need a religion *about* Jesus, but the religion *of* Jesus.

JN: So happy is the lion which is eaten by the man, for the lion becomes the man; and cursed is the man who is eaten by the lion, for the man becomes lion.

SP: You're saying be careful whom we join with; for good or ill, they will shape us? I note that you've always avoided allegiance to any particular Pharisean schools, keeping apart from all of them. We like to join with others, but sometimes others aren't good for us, perhaps? So where do we live from?

JN: My followers asked me this. They said, 'Teach us about the place where you dwell for we must seek it?'

SP: Now that's the question. What did you say to them?

JN: There is light within people of light, and they shine it upon the whole world.

SP: We have light within us? You have light, we have light. It can't be that simple.

JN: Have faith in God, for aren't five sparrows sold for a penny?

SP: But what have sparrows got to do with our inner life?

JN: Not one of them falls to the ground without your father's consent.

SP: And is that so reassuring?

JN: You are of more value than many sparrows.

SP: Yes, but so were you, teacher, and you were killed.

JN: Hah! Do not be afraid of those who kill the body, but are not able to kill the soul –

SP: – or kill the light? Sometimes I meet people in whom the light has been killed, teacher. I think circumstances can do that to people or people can do that to people. Somehow the light within us is extinguished by our experiences; we lose it along the way. Can we get it back?

JN: What parent is there who, if their son asked for bread, would give him a stone?

SP: How do you mean?

JN: Or if he asks for a fish, will give him a snake?

SP: Are you asking us to trust?

JN: If you who are bad still know how to give good gifts to
your children, then how much more will your father in heaven
give good things to those who ask him?

SP: I don't like to be called 'bad' but maybe you're right.
We're brutalized by life, I suppose; and our goodness is folded
up and put away. We give most of our time to primal needs
like survival and self-aggrandizement. And, in such a fragile
psychic state, when we're threatened or hurt, trust can depart
as quickly as the desert mist.

JN: So be merciful, even as your father is also merciful.

SP: And thus complete the circle of divine kindness? Here is
harmony and strength.

JN: Don't judge, and you won't be judged.

SP: Remove my judge's wig?

JN: Don't condemn, and you won't be condemned.

SP: Condemnation, discreet or otherwise, is my daily fare,
teacher; but I can see how it saps the soul, diminishes the light,
and sends me further into a wilderness of despair.

JN: Set free and you will be set free.

SP: Indeed, though surely there's an irony here? For religion,
as you know well, often uses God to do the precise things you

153

have just warned me against! It uses God to judge, God to condemn and God to shackle. Religions have almost taught the world about these arts.

JN: Don't think that I came to destroy the law or the prophets.

SP: You may not have come to destroy them, teacher, but believe me, they look very different in your hands. I don't hear John the Baptizer ever saying what you just said: 'Set free, and you will be set free.'

JN: I didn't come to destroy, but to fulfil.

SP: But you do destroy. You dismantle the law, you dismantle each of us, you expose our intentions and leave us as nothing, beggars by the side of the road. You ask too much honesty of us; and we are not used to honesty.

JN: But no one who puts his hand to the plough and looks back is fit for the kingdom.

SP: No. And so like the seed, we can only become something, when we've become nothing? Is that what you're saying? Until then, we're too well-defended.

JN: Blessed are the poor in spirit, yes.

SP: Until such time, our experiences of life don't penetrate deeply enough to change us. We don't allow them to change us, as perhaps your time in the wilderness changed you? You want to stir these deep energies in us, energies which find meaning in the moment, and make us as you are?

JN: No pupil is greater than his teacher, but when they have completed their training, they will be like their teacher, yes.

SP: It seems you don't want a religious person, teacher, you want a new person, and this cannot be achieved by outer compulsion – by rule, regulation, belief, or threat. Somehow the individual must see, receive, understand, and apply truth to themselves.

JN: How happy are those who receive the word of God and obey it!

SP: You know what worries me, teacher?

JN: Have anxiety about nothing.

SP: I worry for the time when people think they own you.

JN: Hah! Listen, there was once a man who went out early in the morning to hire some men to work in his vineyard.

SP: But don't you see how dangerous this sense of ownership might be?

JN: The vineyard owner agreed to pay them the going rate, a silver coin a day, and off they went to work.

SP: I submit to the story.

JN: Then at nine o'clock, he went out again into the market-place and saw men with time on their hands, so he said to them, 'You too go and work in the vineyard and I'll pay you fairly.' And so they joined the other workers in the vineyard.

SP: And it's hard and hot work. I've done it myself.

JN: And then the owner did the same thing again at midday and three o'clock –

SP: – more recruiting –

JN: – and then at five o'clock, he went to the marketplace again, and said to those standing there, 'Why are you wasting the whole day here doing nothing? You can also go and work in the vineyard if you wish.'

SP: Rather late in the day; but time for an hour's work, I suppose.

JN: Now when evening came, the owner told the foreman to pay the men their wages, and those who started at five o'clock were paid a silver coin each.

SP: A silver coin for an hour's work? I foresee trouble.

JN: And yes, when those who were hired first came to be paid, they thought they would get more.

SP: But they didn't, did they? And they were furious!

JN: 'These men worked only one hour,' they grumbled, 'while we endured a whole day in the hot sun – and yet we find ourselves paid the same!'

SP: I can feel their discomfort.

JN: Listen friend, said the owner, I haven't cheated you. After all, you agreed a day's work for a silver coin. Don't I have the right to do as I wish with my own money? Or are you upset because I am generous?

SP: You *do* agree with me. There's no agreement that ties God to any one person or group. God's generosity spills everywhere! You yourself came for the lost house of Israel, but found the house got larger and larger.

JN: There are many rooms in my father's house, yes. So give, and it will be given to you.

SP: Be generous in attitude, and discover generosity?

JN: Good measure, pressed down, shaken together, and running over will be given to you. For with the same measure you measure, so will it be measured back to you.

SP: And you now, teacher? What does the future hold for you?

JN: I have come from the father and have come into the world; and now I am leaving the world and going to the father.

SP: And us? I mean your followers are asking. How should we fast? How should we pray? How should we give alms? What rules of diet should we follow?

JN: Stop lying.

SP: Stop lying?

JN: Stop lying.

SP: I lie too much, it's true; I lie to myself mostly. Because reality appears unloving, we fall asleep to reality, and create for ourselves a smaller setting in which to survive.

JN: Then do not do that which is against your love –

SP: – that which is less than generous?

JN: You are naked before heaven, so what you hide will be revealed, and whatever is covered, will be uncovered.

SP: You invite us to be like a clear spring day, when all is seen quite plainly.

JN: And as I've said, when you bring forth that within you, then that will save you; if you do not, then that will kill you.

SP: We are to draw deep from our own well, where there is sweet water. You certainly have no desire to create dependence, do you? Some like dependent followers, but not you.

JN: *You* are the light of the world.

SP: Really?

JN: Listen, if the body has come into being because of the spirit, it is a marvel; but if the spirit has come into being because of the body, it is a marvel of marvels. But as for me, I marvel at this: how this great wealth has settled in this poverty.

SP: Yet for much of the time, our wealth is hidden and our poverty is all we reveal. We fear the darkness, and so we never find the light. You appear to be different. You went there, you journeyed to the heart of darkness; but without your trust, we're not so brave. You reach into an unknown part of us and say 'Go there;' but an iron band of fear holds us back.

JN: Don't be alarmed.

SP: Darkness is alarming.

JN: Become as a child, and love your brother and sister as your soul; keep them as the apple of your eye.

SP: Return to the time when there was no iron band? Is that possible?

JN: The one who is faithful in a little, is faithful in much.

SP: That's encouraging. We start from where we are, and do what we can, yes. And in a way, we've come the full circle, teacher, for this is where we started. We started with a child and have ended with one, so perhaps we're done with words. There's nothing to learn but trust; and nothing I need know but my own innocence, and therefore the innocence of others. This is what sitting with you has revealed.

JN: It is impossible for anyone to see the everlasting reality and not become like it.

SP: This conversation, teacher, it is finished, I sense it. You've sat here in the shadows of the tent, offering yourself, but now, strange, it's as though you're already gone.

JN: I must be about my father's business.

SP: Of course. So is this goodbye?

JN: Split the wood and I am there. Turn over the stone, and

there you will find me.

SP: And that's enough.

Reflections from the marketplace

It seemed appropriate to just get up and leave the table. Whatever Jesus had been like before his death, there is an unreachable quality to him now; intimate but unreachable. As he had said to even his closest friend, Mary: 'Do not touch me.'

What am I to make of my conversation? Initially, my head is full of the pictures he draws from nature and life. The world is indeed his scripture. I see the lilies of the field, the patient farmer, the suspect builder, the solitary seed, the angry man woken at midnight, the falling sparrows, and the deaths in Siloam. He uses whatever is around him to say truthful things. And such a sense of humour! I still smile when I think of the man with the beam in his eye advising his friend about the speck in his. And what did he write in the sand when the woman caught in adultery was brought to him? I now wish I'd asked.

So who is Jesus? Here is a man of great courage; that comes before almost anything else. A man who declined both the comforts of home and the goodwill of his family to become a wandering preacher. What did he preach? It was nothing new in a way; and yet, it was entirely new. He talked of trust, as witnessed most clearly in a child; of humble prayer purified by our forgiveness of others; and of the fatherhood of God – an intimate fatherhood, defined by the word 'daddy'. No other teacher I have ever heard has suggested this. And no other teacher has told us to love our enemies.

From these deep springs emerges a kingdom where all are healed, where tears are wiped from our eyes, and a new sense of family exists, more generous and open than our present partial understanding.

Oh, and the way he uses language! The verbal twists, the stories, the hyperbole, the savagery, and the satire – he's like a butterfly, determined never to be pinned down, but always to provoke and shatter so a new climate of learning is made possible. He'd call that preparation for the kingdom. And so he dismantles our certainties, pierces our pomposity, overturns our past, confuses our pathways, ridicules our sacred, and leaves us naked – because to become naked is to unlearn everything we thought we knew.

He can't share his understanding with us, of course; understanding cannot be shared, only discovered by each soul for themselves. But he seems to imagine that such discovery is possible. It's as if he says, 'That which is alive in me, is alive also in you, but I can't take you there.' It may mean us changing our mind; but Jesus was courageous enough to change his mind along the way – remember the woman in Tyre? – proving the old saying: 'Life is change and to be perfect is to have changed often.'

As I leave the marketplace, and walk down towards the temple, I reflect also on his lack of sentimentality. No one is more aware than Jesus of the destructive forces at work in the world; and more particularly, in individual people. Everyone is potentially lethal. And knowing the power and presence of such dark forces in each human soul, his language about them is savage. He links intention to action, motive with deed, leaving no one safe. So no, he colludes with nothing that has left the place of light, and this has lost him many friends, and made him many enemies.

As a consequence, he struggles to be heard; people fear him and turn on him. And as the story of the four soils reveals, for much of the time his message cannot penetrate through our barriers of habitual reaction. It is hardly surprising that he was crucified; he threatens everyone – except children.

He doesn't want us to take ourselves too seriously, of course, a frequent failing in adults. His stories are full of people taking themselves too seriously and getting upset accordingly. Instead, he wants us to repent into a new mind, a new way of experiencing things – a way of life that is full of trust and therefore quite free of anxiety. What happened to Zacchaeus, I wonder, after his encounter with Jesus? It's a new way of being that does not draw all its meaning from outer events, but is at heart an inner event, an inner state which is the kingdom of God within, merciful towards others and freeing of others, for that is how God is to us.

It is strange that a message of such kindness draws Jesus into such conflict, but that perhaps says more about us than him. It's a sad fact that goodness does not always bring forth goodness; that sometimes it brings forth hate. But the more I reflect on the man, the simpler he becomes. Has he in fact done anything more than restore us to our lost parentage, to an intimacy we've been hardened against? In my travels, I've been advised to follow the wise, the intelligent, and the awakened; 'follow them as the moon follows the path of the stars,' I have been told. And Jesus seems to be such a man.

I look back only once as I walk away. I see Jesus in the doorway of the tent – I think it's Jesus – paying the girl who had been serving us throughout the evening. I'd forgotten all about her, and I did think of going back, but it seemed Jesus was sorting things.

The End

Paperbacks also available from White Crow Books

Lucius Annaeus Seneca—*On Benefits*
ISBN 978-1-907355-19-6

Rebecca Ruter Springer—*Intra Muros—My Dream of Heaven*
ISBN 978-1-907355-11-0

W. T. Stead—*After Death or Letters from Julia: A Personal Narrative*
ISBN 978-1-907355-89-9

Leo Tolstoy, edited by Simon Parke—*Forbidden Words*
ISBN 978-1-907355-00-4

Leo Tolstoy—*A Confession*
ISBN 978-1-907355-24-0

Leo Tolstoy—*The Gospel in Brief*
ISBN 978-1-907355-22-6

Leo Tolstoy—*The Kingdom of God is Within You*
ISBN 978-1-907355-27-1

Leo Tolstoy—*My Religion: What I Believe*
ISBN 978-1-907355-23-3

Leo Tolstoy—*On Life*
ISBN 978-1-907355-91-2

Leo Tolstoy—*Twenty-three Tales*
ISBN 978-1-907355-29-5

Leo Tolstoy—*What is Religion and other writings*
ISBN 978-1-907355-28-8

Leo Tolstoy—*Work While Ye Have the Light*
ISBN 978-1-907355-26-4

Leo Tolstoy with Simon Parke—*Conversations with Tolstoy*
ISBN 978-1-907355-25-7

Vincent Van Gogh with Simon Parke—*Conversations with Van Gogh*
ISBN 978-1-907355-95-0

Howard Williams with an Introduction by Leo Tolstoy—*The Ethics of Diet: An Anthology of Vegetarian Thought*
ISBN 978-1-907355-21-9

Allan Kardec—*The Spirits Book*
ISBN 978-1-907355-98-1

Wolfgang Amadeus Mozart with Simon Parke—*Conversations with Mozart*
ISBN 978-1-907661-38-9

Jesus of Nazareth with Simon Parke—*Conversations with Jesus of Nazareth*
ISBN 978-1-907661-41-9

Rudolf Steiner—*Christianity as a Mystical Fact: And the Mysteries of Antiquity*
ISBN 978-1-907661-52-5

Thomas à Kempis with Simon Parke—*The Imitation of Christ*
ISBN 978-1-907661-58-7

Emanuel Swedenborg—*Heaven and Hell*
ISBN 978-1-907661-55-6

P.D. Ouspensky—*Tertium Organum: The Third Canon of Thought*
ISBN 978-1-907661-47-1

Dwight Goddard—*The Buddhist Bible*
ISBN 978-1-907661-44-0

Leo Tolstoy—*The Death of Ivan Ilyich*
ISBN 978-1-907661-10-5

Leo Tolstoy—*Resurrection*
ISBN 978-1-907661-09-9

All titles available as eBooks, and selected titles available in Hardback and Audiobook formats from www.whitecrowbooks.com